Praise for Beyond a Charmed Life

"Barb is a visionary. Where others see struggle, she sees hope." **—Matt Seubert, Associate Executive Director for Development, AccessCNY**

"Barb Tresness is a tireless advocate for the rights of people with disabilities, and she's a champion for ensuring equality in communication." **—Peter Blanck, Ph.D., J.D., Chairman, Burton Blatt Institute & University Professor, Syracuse University**

"I remember vividly how she spoke up, 'Just because Graham cannot speak directly to you with words does not mean that he has any less pride in himself as a person and young man. Please respect him as you work with him.' And she was the living embodiment of that respect—she was not just his mother, she was always his defender, his coach and his partner." **—William M. Cunningham, (retired CranioSacral Therapist)**

"As long as I have known her, Barb has been highly committed and dedicated to educating everyone who interacts with Graham. She is a passionate advocate for those who cannot speak for themselves." **—Beth Tollar, M.S., CCC-SLP/L, NYS Licensed Speech-Language Pathologist**

"Barb dedicates her work in the world to those who have communication challenges and those who may learn to communicate with them." **—Kat Perry, CranioSacral Therapist CST-D, Integrative Intentions, LLC, Upledger Institute International**

"Barb is connected and understands the importance of voice and being heard, whatever way that happens to be."
—Glenda Greenberg, LMT, CranioSacral Therapist, Dolphin Assisted Therapy Program, Upledger Institute International

"With her creative imagination, Barb is educating the public on how to communicate with people who are nonverbal."
—Kate Battoe, Research Assistant at the Burton Blatt Institute

"Barb's leadership and education are enriching lives and creating truly inclusive community in which all voices are heard. Her innovative approach is life changing."
—Prudence York, Executive Director, AccessCNY

"Graham's story and the unending support he gets from Barb will always make him one of my best teachers. My son told me when he was small, that children choose their parents before they come in, if so then Graham certainly knew what he was doing when he chose Barb!" **—Carol McLellan, CranioSacral Therapist CST-D, CPO-D, Ombudsman CCPB Upledger Institute International**

"There is a saying that things work out best for those who make the best of how things work out. To me, this means that regardless of the circumstances you may face in life, you can either commiserate as a victim or strive to be a champion. While it is easy to say you prefer to be a champion, the path to get there is not always clear or without great effort. In this book, Barb shows by her own personal life experience how those facing even the most adverse and trying situations can find their way out of victim-hood. Barb and her son Graham's journey is truly inspirational and motivating... and you will see how they were able to overcome severe obstacles to become true champions. Kudos to Barb and Graham for sharing their deeply personal and moving story so others can benefit."
—**John Matthew Upledger, CEO, Upledger Institute International**

Kim –

Beyond A Charmed Life

A Mother's Unconditional Love

Barbara Huntress Tresness

Barbara Huntress Tresness

Let Your Love Shine!

DIVINE PHOENIX BOOKS

Divine Phoenix Books
PO Box 1001
Skaneateles. NY, 13152
www.divinephoenixbooks.com

First Edition: December 2015

Published in North America by Divine Phoenix and Pegasus Books. For information, please contact Divine Phoenix c/o Laura Ponticello, PO Box 1001, Skaneateles, NY, 13152.

This book is a work of creative nonfiction. The events are portrayed to the best of Barbara Huntress Tresness' memory. While all the stories in the book are true and author tried to portray events as accurately as possible, at times scenes or conversations might be condensed or paraphrased. Given each person may remember incidences and occurrences differently; this is the Author's story.

Library of Congress Cataloguing-In-Publication Data
Barbara Huntress Tresness
Beyond A Charmed Life/ Barbara Huntress Tresness 1st ed
p. cm.
Library of Congress Control Number: 2015956267
ISBN - 978-1-941859-43-8

1.BIOGRAPHIES & AUTOBIOGRAPHY / Personal Memoirs. 2. FAMILY & RELATIONSHIPS / Parenting. 3. FAMILY & RELATIONSHIPS / Special Needs. 4. BODY, MIND & SPIRIT / Inspiration & Personal Growth. 5. SELF-HELP / General. 6. BODY, MIND & SPIRIT / Healing / General.

10   9   8   7   6   5   4   3   2   1

Comments about *Beyond A Charmed Life* and requests for additional copies, book club rates and author speaking appearances may be addressed to Barbara Huntress Tresness at CHAT Collective, 100 Clinton Street, Fayetteville, NY 13066 and www.chatcollective.com.
Chris Moebs, Interior Book Design & Production, Pegasus Books
Photo credit, dedication page, Robert Carroll Photography
Photo credit, author photo and scrapbook photos, Lydia Johnson Grandy, Johnson Camera

Also available as an eBook from Internet retailers, author's website and from Divine Phoenix Books

Printed in the United States of America

To my guys, Greg, Colby, Tysen and Graham: I love you with all my heart!

What Happens When You Search For Hope?

Sharing our stories out loud helped me and helped others. It got easier as I began to tell some of what had happened to us. I kept many journals and wrote about my feelings, good and bad. I never wanted Graham to think he was difficult for us to care for. I wanted him to know he was loved unconditionally.

—Barbara Huntress Tresness

Beyond a Charmed Life, A Mother's Unconditional Love is an inspirational memoir about a mother's love for her special needs son, with heartfelt stories and a triumphant spirit of overcoming insurmountable challenges. From caretaker to advocate role, Barb wants to share "you are not alone and hope does exist". This is a story of tenacity, triumph and a spiritual awakening to the universal forces that help mother and child have an unbroken bond that transcends everything.

Beyond A Charmed Life

Barbara Huntress Tresness

Table of Contents

A Note from the Author

When Graham was born we did not have a diagnosis and I would not allow myself to think anything about him was difficult. That felt like a betrayal of sorts. He did not do anything wrong. I would not admit that I was struggling or that our life was challenging because of him. It took me years to accept the thought that our life would have been so much easier if Graham did not come into it the way he had.

Sharing our stories out loud helped me and helped others. It got easier as I began to tell some of what had happened to us. I kept many journals and wrote about my feelings good and bad. I never wanted Graham to think he was difficult for us to care for. I wanted him to know he was loved unconditionally. As he grew into a confident young man I realized he was able to hear about his story.

I had no idea how emotional it would be for me to read it to him. Sharing my fears and struggles about him out loud was a beautiful part of our journey together. We sat under the wisteria vines in our yard together and I read it all to him. I planted those vines when he was born and they grew into a beautiful place for us to share together.

I would not print anything Graham did not approve of. He had to hear it all and I asked him after each chapter what he thought. I cried a lot as I read this to him. He was serious during the tough parts but there was joy and laughter too. Graham knows our stories were meant to be shared and he is ready to do that.

To all the families out there struggling like our family struggled, I want you to know this: You will survive it. It hurts. I cried every day. It consumed my life. It was a pain I could not shake. I would console myself that as long as we moved forward in any way, no matter how small, that we made a difference. It is a horrible feeling not to be able to help your child. To stop the pain. To see them treated unjustly.

It's a familiar phrase: welcome to my world. It's often said when someone is bitter, resentful, or sarcastic. It's almost as if there is no way you could really understand my world or what I am going through. That's what this is all about. It's Graham's world really and sharing our journey has made an impact through the years.

There is a feeling of complete isolation that goes with many things: disease, disability, depression. Telling our stories--Graham's and mine--has brought hope and inspiration to many people just in conversations. It is time to take our stories to the next level. To let people know they are not alone or isolated in what they are going through.

We all struggle with something. Up until my third son was born, my struggles were minor.

The cover of this book is a photo of Graham and me in Freeport Bahamas. It was dusk in the infinity pool and it was as if we were alone at the ocean together. It's as if Graham and I are suspended in the water, time stops and in that moment, our love transcends it all.

My children are grown up now and my job as their mother has changed. At this turning point in my life I am looking forward to watching my three sons and their own journeys as they head out on their own to live their own lives. I know they will be successful whatever they do!

Without words my son Graham has touched so many lives in his fifteen years. His is a remarkable journey that I am happy to tell. I hope you enjoy our stories... Barb

What if you had always led a charmed life? Everything was easy for you. You grew up on "the right side of the tracks," your family had money, and you wanted for nothing. Your parents paid for college and even gave you a car to drive. You met a boy, fell in love and got married. You bought a house, started a family in a beautiful suburban town, had lots of friends and life was good.

You were the mom that was the room mom at school, the one who made special cakes for the kids' birthdays and brought holiday themed goodies to school. You volunteered in your community, went to lots of parties and fundraisers, and your husband was successful and you could travel and see the world.

It was a charmed life.
Until the day it was not.

Prologue:

Beyond my grasp

When you have a baby you do everything for it, from feeding, to changing, to bathing... and you love doing it. But usually the baby grows to learn to do those things for him or herself. That did not happen with Graham, so year after many years I was still feeding, changing and bathing him-- and it was much harder to do with a ten-year-old.

It took ten years for me to get Graham into a full day summer program so I could sit in a lawn chair in my bathing suit and begin to write this memoir. It took that long for me to have the awareness that it is okay to focus on me. I was mom first. Barb disappeared when Graham needed me to be more than his mom: a full time caregiver of a child with severe needs was my new role. I remember wondering out loud what normal people do during the summer.

When Graham was 10, I had my first break from my role as full time caregiver. It was summer and the first time I had time by myself in over a decade. That may be hard for you to relate to, but I always had Graham with me or on my mind. It was finally okay to just be. I know he's okay and I am too.
When the world you live in turns upside down, none of the little stuff matters anymore. Yet life goes on, and you have to pretend to care about things that might have been significant in your life if it hadn't been turned upside down: Like a child not making a sports team, or a friend that complains about colic when your child hasn't slept through the night in seven years. What about us? Can't anyone see our struggle?

Turns out, they could not.

Sure, people get that it's hard. It's hard. What does that mean actually? The part they don't get is the 24/7 piece. Day after day, week after week, month after month, year after year. It's why writing this book is important. So that the world can get it, and others who struggle like our family will know they are not alone. The little things in life fall away, and your priorities get rearranged fast.

Caring for Graham impacted our lives in large and small ways. The multiple therapists and doctors we now had to interact with was overwhelming. The Early Intervention program director told me she talked about our family often as an example of what not to do.

Each therapist came to our house two or three times per week, and there were five of them. That is ten to fifteen visits each week, and during each visit the well-meaning therapist would ask me to do something. All five of them had a "To Do" list for me every time they came to our house, and there was no physical way I could do it all.

The physical therapist wanted me to stretch him and practice rolling and strengthening exercises. The speech therapist had games and activities for us to do. The occupational therapist said he should be in the therapy swing every day and gave me exercises to work on relaxing the muscles inside his mouth. They told us to learn sign language. My head was spinning. That doesn't include the multiple doctors we saw and what they wanted us to do. Oh and he needed our help eating, moving and toileting too.

The medical community involved in guiding our family did not collaborate with each other, and each office had their own set of things we had to do—in addition to what the therapists wanted us to do. To say that we were overwhelmed doesn't quite cut it. I felt lost, alone, helpless. The list of things to do made it harder. We felt guilty we could not do it all. Why wasn't anyone able to help us?

A family member reminded me of something I had told her years ago. "You once said to me, 'If I had twelve children it still wouldn't be as much work as having one like Graham.'"

"I did?" I asked.

"Yes, you did," they said.

I guess I did. I was right.

Chapter One

Beyond my worst nightmare: his birth

Graham is nonverbal. He cannot use his voice to speak. I had never met anyone who could not talk before. It is so hard to imagine how frustrating it would be not to be able to talk. When Graham is hurt he cannot tell me where or what hurts him. All he can do is cry.

Understanding his cries would be the first step in healing for me. Through CranioSacral Therapy, or CST—a gentle touch therapy—I learned that crying is communication. By listening to the cries, I learned there were differences between them.

One cry sounded sad, another like a yearning for something. Another cry was consoling, when he was trying to go to sleep. And then I could hear the scared cry, or the one that pierced my ears and made my blood run cold: pain or terror. Sometimes I could figure out what I thought he wanted or needed, and sometimes I could not.

For his first six years we had gone through anguish, pain and hurt. There were times when he cried out, and I longed to help him but didn't know how. Here is an example: To bed at 9 o'clock, up screaming at 10, 12 and 1 am. The 1 am was the worst until the gas passed through his body. I could hear it, and I felt his pain. I heard his cries of pain. I did not know how to help. I was sad for him, mad for him. When would it end?

It was beyond cruel. No one signs on for the heartbreak part. It happened over and over again. Day after day, week after week, month after month. Initially it was a grieving process, then that painful feeling happened at specific events: birthday parties, school events, report cards, times when the challenges were so obvious that it hurt. When people stared or said something stupid you were brought down again. I had no idea how bad it could get.

Who is he? Graham Chamberlain Tresness was born May 1, 2000. I began writing this book after a decade of devotion to Graham: a decade of my life, a decade of challenge, a decade of survival, a decade of tears. A Decade. Where did it go?

I've been in survival mode since my placenta abrupted on May 1, 2000. My life turned upside-down. Graham has multiple disabilities. He has cerebral palsy, is nonverbal, non- ambulatory, has a bilateral hearing loss and cortical visual impairment. Has it really been a decade? How did I do it? It is almost feels like another lifetime. So much pain, so many stories, and yet here we are. We made it.

At age 10 for Graham, I did not have to worry anymore. Let me restate that. Parents always worry: it's our job. But not at the non-stop level of panic and fear I had been worrying at. I could dial it down. He was finally seen by the world the way I had always seen him.

Each time I've shared one small story about Graham, I've seen the impact our experiences have made on the faces of those who are listening. I am continually amazed at how much of a difference one person's life has made on this world we live in, and all without words.

Daily I see wondrous things occur just by knowing Graham. Lives changed just by his smile alone. You could say that many feel grateful for their own lives when they see someone less fortunate than they are. This is different. This child has changed the world. He did it in silence. He continues silently touching lives.

The Graham effect: without words, this child has impacted lives around the world. His presence has taught all of us how important our connections in this life truly are.

I love you, Graham!

Let me tell you how it all started.

Greg and I met in October of 1983 our freshman year of college at the University of Vermont (UVM). We were together all four years of college. We traveled together during college breaks, our families were together at graduation and while we each moved home for a bit after college, we knew we would be together soon. We married in 1991 and moved to his hometown, Manlius, New York to raise a family.

Our first baby was born in 1995 at 10 pounds, 10 ounces. Colby James Tresness. Colby started preschool and never looked back. He would always say, "I hope you have a happy day" when he left for school. He loved being at school and still does: He received many academic awards, and he is now a Junior at Brown University in Providence, Rhode Island.

Tysen was born in 1997 at 8 pounds, 6 ounces three weeks early. He had a ball in his hands as soon as he could hold one and has always loved sports. He had a head full of blonde "curlies." He started school at four, turning five a month into kindergarten. He would always be on the younger side of his peers, and yet he excelled at school, in all honors classes just like his big brother.

Tysen achieved his dream and was named an All American Soccer Player in 2014 as a senior captain of his undefeated team. Only 57 players received this honor. In June of 2015 he was also recognized as a Scholar All American Athlete. Only 33 players received this honor. He put academics first and achieved honors in both areas. Both my boys received recognition from the State of New York as AP Scholars with Distinction/Honor.

Graham was born in 2000, and we almost lost him. He has multiple disabilities and is fully dependent on others for his care. While he had a rough start to his life, he has managed to have a positive outlook. I challenge anyone to be in the same room with him when he is laughing and contain your own smile.

He has a way of cheering anyone up with a flash of that smile, or the full body smile and giggle. It is crazy to think that he is a teenager, weighing in at 75 pounds and a little hair on his lip... how can that be! His voice is deeper, but the laughter is still contagious.

I turned 50 in 2014. Both my parents have passed away, and my boys have grown up. Tysen is at college this fall attending the University of Virginia (UVA) and it is just Greg, Graham and me. Going through 14 years of scrapbooks to put together a timeline for this book was difficult and wonderful all at the same time.

We had a wonderful life raising our three boys with lots of happy memories. As I wrote the finishing pages of this book in Aspen Colorado, and Nantucket Massachusetts, I appreciated the beauty of nature surrounding me and realized that our family experiences, both good and bad, made for an incredible journey together.

Chapter Two

Beyond my charmed life

My first two children were born with blonde hair and blue eyes. We named them Colby and Tysen. Life was good. We took them to Disney World when they each turned five, and I was pregnant with my third child on our first trip. We went for Thanksgiving with both sets of grandparents.

We were the picture perfect American family. Our world centered around our children. We unknowingly named our first two sons after foods. I had never heard of Colby cheese or Tyson chicken. My biggest concern when Tysen was born was that a prize fighter had bit another fighter's ear off, and would that somehow stick with my baby if I named him Tysen? Little did I know what worried could mean.

I was jarred awake by a trickling sensation in my groin. Something was wrong. I fumbled in the dark to make my way to the bathroom. I barely made it before I had the sensation that my water broke...but suddenly I felt woozy. I grabbed the shelf to steady myself, turned on the light and saw the bright red blood in the toilet. I screamed for my husband, and the sheer terror on his face as he saw the bright red toilet bowl mirrored my own fear. He dialed the doctor and handed me the phone. I dropped it as I filled the toilet with blood again, and I almost passed out.

It felt like an eternity had passed as we waited to leave for the hospital. We were standing in the back hall by the door in our coats, waiting. My in-laws were on their way to stay with our other two boys. I was angry that they took so long to get to our house because I knew something was wrong. "What took you so long?" I yelled as they walked through the back door. I was agitated that I knew something was wrong and no one was listening to me.

"You will be fine," they said.

Those words cut right through me.

The voice inside my head disagreed. I was not fine, and neither was my baby. No one listened. The doctor had said on the phone that she would have NICU in the delivery room as a precaution. We asked if we should go by ambulance and were told a car would be fine. I do not like the word fine.

At the emergency room, I was in a wheelchair. I could feel the blood still coming and yelled that I was bleeding and needed help to anyone who would listen. The registration staff person said, "That happens when you have a baby, honey—you're fine." I screamed at her too. "This is my third child, you idiot. Something is wrong!" and then to my husband, "Wheel me to the doctor NOW!"

We got to a room, and I was hooked up to the monitors. Where was the doctor? No answer. A resident came in to examine me, and I asked him where my doctor was. I felt like he put his entire arm, right up to his shoulder, inside me, and I screamed in pain. He went white and ran out of the room. Where was my doctor, and why did that hurt so much? What had he done to me? Did he hurt my baby? Soon they put an oxygen mask on me...but still no doctor.

Still not fine.

When the doctor finally showed up (we later learned the doctor arrived at the hospital and before she checked on me, she went to sleep, telling the staff not to wake her), she yelled from the doorway, still having no examination, "Let's get this show on the road" and staff began wheeling me to the delivery room for surgery. Still not emergency surgery, they stopped to give me drugs. An epidural in the spinal column, which is something you do when there is not an emergency.

I have no idea how long it took for the delivery. Time blurred. When she pulled my son out her words cut right through me. "He's puny," she said with little to no regard for how that would feel to me. Then NICU stepped in, and the baby was taken away to another floor. My husband went with the baby. I was alone in the delivery room in my gown, wondering where my child was going and if he would be okay.

The doctor's callous comment echoed in my head as I lay there shivering. I didn't know if my baby would live or die. I suddenly thought of parents who lost a child. Many had to give birth to a stillborn. In that moment I connected to the horror of thinking your child was dead.

NICU (Neo Natal Intensive Care Unit)

Greg was not allowed to stay past calling hours. He had to leave me alone in the maternity ward. He called the hospital and made the nurses take me to see the baby the night he was born. You are not supposed to get out of bed that quickly after a C-section, but he pleaded with them to let me see my baby in case he didn't make it through the night. It hurt like hell, but the alternative—the possibility of never seeing my baby if he died—pushed me to go.

It hurt to move, let alone walk, but I had to be strong for my baby. I needed to see him in case he died. My baby might not make it through the night. He was in trouble, and I needed to be there for him. I was terrified but focused on each step.

It was eerily quiet when we got to NICU. Big steel doors, beeping monitors. I felt like I was in a movie walking into a strange unfamiliar place.

Then I saw him.

He was so tiny, and he was hooked up to wires with tubing in his nose so he could breathe. He was in a plastic box, and I could not touch him. I cringed looking at him...not the beautiful memory of when you first see your newborn that I had with my first two children. I saw pain and uncertainty as I stared at this baby in a box. How could I help him? I felt helpless. I cried and told him I loved him and to be strong.

He made it through the night. I didn't sleep at all. I remember staring at the hospital tower lit up outside my window, listening to other babies crying, terrified that my child would die...and painfully aware that I was alone and my baby couldn't be with me in this room. Shouldn't there be a separate area for women who were going through this? Walking back from the NICU, I saw another woman walking down the hall cradling her healthy newborn, and her eyes met mine. I quickly looked away, fighting back my tears. My heart ached.

Graham was in the hospital for 23 days. If I knew that after 24 days you qualify or nursing care at home I would have pushed to keep him there. Why did the staff release him before we qualified? We wanted to get out of that place so badly that as soon as they said we could leave, we did. We didn't know any better. It was the first of many situations we would face where not knowing could hurt us or Graham.

We started in the most critical section in the NICU. Those were the babies fighting to survive. The baby next to Graham weighed only one pound and did not even look human to me, I remember thinking that a pound of hamburger looked bigger than what I was looking at. It seemed alien. *How horrible that I am comparing this human being to hamburger,* I thought. I had no frame of reference and no control over my fears.

At one point Greg and I tried to start a conversation with some of the other parents. The nurse on call told us to respect the other family's space and not talk to them while they were with their children. In this section there was no guarantee the baby would make it. We each had our own fears, each child fighting their own separate battle to survive.

We all silently feared the worst. The child next to us who weighed only a pound made Graham seem like a heavyweight champ at 4 pounds, 6 ounces. Isolation from others as well as each other hurt as Greg and I each tried to face this on our own.

No one would tell us what to expect. The NICU, filled with wonderful professional and caring doctors, offered no outlook at all. When asked point blank "Does my child have cerebral palsy?" the doctor from the Neurology Department answered, "Oh, we won't know the answer to that for at least two years."

What? Anyone who has a child will know that is an eternity to wait. So much happens in those early years that it was simply an unacceptable answer. Did they really expect us to wait? Who could wait years for answers? It was cruel to expect us to.

In the year 2000, our lives changed when our baby almost died at birth. Our little fighter hung on and spent the first 23 days of his life in NICU. No one would give us any answers as to what the future would hold. All we heard from the doctors was "it's too early to know." One actually said he didn't know if he would go to Harvard. What a jerk.

We couldn't hold him or hear him. Graham didn't cry for the first seven days of his life. We knew something was very wrong. He had seizures in the NICU, and as a result would spend the first year of his life on a seizure medication, a barbiturate. (In hindsight, we now believe the drug was responsible for his later irritability, constant crying and lack of sleep.) As you can imagine, he was a different child off the drugs. We finally got to see him smile, but not until 14 months later.

During the first few months of Graham's life we were in the crisis mode—and visits to the neurologist, gastroenterologist, audiologist, and ophthalmologist brought little news. We knew something was very wrong, but no one could tell us what. It was all confusing. Getting him to all these appointments, retelling his birth story, the blank faces of doctors and nurses that did not help us was exhausting.

The medical update: let's start with his vision. At two months old, we were told Graham was blind, and he was registered for the Institute for the Blind. He could track with his eyes. He followed toys. We did not believe what this doctor said. He had assured me the eye exam would not hurt. Then he did something to Graham's eye and blood spurted out. "That looks painful to me," I yelled in horror. Graham was a baby, but when they pried his eye open it was the size of an adult's eye. I can still see it today. A big adult eye underneath the eyelids of a baby. I shuddered.

The first doctor told me in front of my son, Tysen, that Graham was blind and there was nothing he could do for him. I could not control the tears, and I came out of the exam room crying. I called Greg's office, but he was not there. The person who answered quickly realized I was hysterical and promised to find Greg and have him call me. I had no control over my emotions. I was hysterical.

I got in the car to drive home, which I never should have done in that state of mind. Tysen helped me keep it together by asking a million questions, as toddlers do. I was trying to see through my tears and suddenly focused on the car logo in front of me. It was an Audi. Greg drove an Audi. I felt comforted.

My eyes slowly left the Audi sign and looked at the driver of the car. It was Greg. I felt a calm wave wash over me. I could follow him home. When we got there, I got out of the car, doubled over in pain and wretched like I would vomit.

He was not blind. He couldn't be. I remember how mad Greg was. I yelled, "You do not get referred to the Institute for the Blind if you need glasses." We learned the hard way not to believe everything you hear. The medical system was not what we thought it should be. We got a second opinion.

We found another doctor who told us that Graham has Cortical Visual Impairment, or CVI, which means sometimes the brain signal to the eye is on and sometimes it is off. However the eye itself looked healthy. This was a neurological condition affecting his vision. Graham was not blind. What a relief.

Feeding was a major issue for Graham right from the start. He was able to nurse (breast milk) with adaptations but he was fussy.We were told Graham was crying all the time because of gastrointestinal problems, such as an allergy to his formula. We tried pretty much every baby formula on the market, finally setting on a prescription formula. After another second and third opinion and minor exploratory surgery, it turned out the problem was reflux, which was controlled effectively with a mild drug.

The good news was that in a very short time Graham was off the bottle and drinking from a big boy cup. He needed someone to hold the cup, but he could drink from it with help. We did not know if he would ever eat independently. One step at a time.

When your family is hurtled into a crisis, you do your best to keep your head above water and survive. When dealing with doctors, therapists, fear, anger, grief—let alone our other children—it's no wonder there was little time to understand all that had happened. You spend your days hoping and praying that your child will beat the odds— that he's different.

You grieve for the perfect child that never came, and you grieve for all that he will never be able to do. You hope—until you're told different—that he can beat this. Then one day a kind, compassionate, renowned doctor gently gives you the formal diagnosis you've known all along but didn't want to hear: Graham has cerebral palsy.

Cerebral palsy is a blanket term used to describe a brain injury. CP is not an illness, and Graham is not sick. The technical term for the type of CP that Graham has is spastic quadriplegia. His brain was damaged, most likely in utero as well as during birth. The injury will not go away. Graham's body just won't let him do the things he wants to do. The reality is that he is a wonderful, happy, adorable child with a disability who has a smile that brightens everyone's day.

The hardest part to hear was that, on a sliding scale, Graham had a very involved case of CP. We were told that, most likely, given the odds, he would never sit or walk unaided. That was a tough nut to swallow...but for us the next one was more difficult. We were told Graham might never be able to speak to us.

Given his moderate hearing loss, his language "input" was impaired. Cerebral palsy causes all kinds of difficulty with muscle control. Graham's tongue and facial muscles are affected, meaning that his language "output" is impaired also. In addition, the ability to speak depends on good posture and trunk control, which Graham also has difficulty with.

That blew me away. *I'm not ready to accept that. I won't do it. He'll find a way. We'll find a way together,* I thought. We knew that it was going to be a long road, but we were very confident that we could positively impact his communications skills.

Physically, Graham was so small when he was born, and he immediately had issues with weight gain. His body was rigid. He would stiffen his body, and we would be unable to bend his arms or legs. We spent the first few months just trying to pacify or console him.

Slowly we realized he could not control his head muscles. His head flopped to his chest like a baby who is tired. That was one of the most frequent comments we'd hear from strangers... "Oh, is he tired? Oh, he looks like he's sleeping."

When Graham was a baby, it was difficult to hold him in a position where he had good head control. He preferred to be held with his back to your tummy—facing out. This does not look like a nurturing position and was difficult for us when he was so unhappy. To the outside world, it must have seemed unnatural and cold-hearted, when in fact, it was the best way to comfort him.

At age two, Graham still could not sit on his own. He would fall over. It became clear that his balance may never be enough for him to achieve independence. He would require 24-hour supervision and special equipment to help him be independent.

We knew it looked like he would need a wheelchair and that walking would not happen independently, but we held out hope that physical therapy might change that. Could he learn things that other kids did, just much slower? This felt better than a life sentence to a chair.

As he grew up, Graham had to work so hard to accomplish the smallest things. At age 5, for Graham to see your hand to give you a "high five," it took so much effort for his brain to get the message to the right muscles and for his arms to try to wind up and take a swing at your hand. It would take three or four times until he actually hit your hand. When he did it, the room would light up and his big brothers would be the first to yell, "He did it!"

Graham started with Early Intervention, a federally funded program, when he was two months old. Graham had six therapists, a neurologist, gastroenterologist, an ophthalmologist and audiologist, as well as a regular pediatrician. In addition to physical therapy, occupational therapy, speech therapy, sensory integration, special education, sign language and auditory therapy, we tried alternative routes to improve the quality of his life. We would have done anything we could to help Graham.

Early on we heard about Hyperbaric Oxygen Treatments (HBOT). The theory is that breathing pure oxygen under pressure helps rejuvenate dormant or damaged brain cells that can be trained to do things that they couldn't do before.

We committed to a monthly trip, and Graham did over 100 "dives" in the Hyperbaric chamber, which kind of looked like a small submarine. Every month we would pack the van, load the kids and drive to Connecticut to go to HBOT. Colby and Tysen had fun taking the trip, and the staff was great with them. As for Graham, he cried a lot during the treatments. He had to wear an oxygen mask over his head, kind of like an astronaut.

During one of our sessions at HBOT, we had a lesson in humanity. There was a child on the ground and one of our older boys lost control of a plastic ball he was playing with and it hit the boy on the floor. I was mortified. I turned red and told him to apologize to the boy. The boy's father said,

"Don't bother apologizing to him, he wouldn't know it if you hit him in the head with a hammer."

I was appalled. You could have heard a pin drop. My son turned and looked at me, and I told him that he was old enough to know the difference between right and wrong and that he should do the right thing. He walked over to the little boy to apologize. I'll never forget it. In my eyes, that father did not see his child as a human being. Gratefully my son did.

We eventually stopped HBOT as we began to see a repetitive movement in Graham after a "dive" that we had not seen before. It felt like a sign to move on, and we did. That is when we found CranioSacral Therapy or (CST).

When Graham was two and a half years old we brought a therapist into our home to do craniosacral therapy. We saw Graham smile for the first time in his life. Up until that point he was a sad, unhappy child. He cried constantly, unable to console or settle himself. Now that we had seen a glimmer of joy, we would not give up until we found out how to get him more smiles. It was impossible to know how he felt until he showed us that smile. He gave us hope.

We would take him to the Bahamas for CST and amazing things happened. I will get to that part of the story but for now, let's get back to the beginning and what we did to survive. We had to tell people what had happened. We wanted to share all of this with our family and friends for several reasons, so we wrote a letter when he was a baby and sent it out to our community. First, selfishly, it was easier than explaining it time and time again to all of our family and friends. It allowed us to focus on current issues instead of updating everyone on where we've been. Anything that simplified life at that point was a necessity!

The second reason was to let people know who Graham was, what he'd been through, all that he had overcome already, and what a long road he had ahead. In our letter we implored them not to feel sorry for Graham, but instead to understand all that he faces daily and to appreciate life in all of its forms. Near the end of the letter we wrote, "It is our hope that, given this knowledge about Graham's disabilities, it will be easier for you to be with him and be comfortable."

In sending the letter, we asked that people should feel free to share it with anyone who may have asked how Graham was doing. We hoped that they would feel comfortable talking to us about this and any other questions they may have had about any of the things we'd shared. They did. It made our lives easier and our friends and relatives more comfortable talking to us about the tough stuff. This wonderful little boy taught us to live our lives for the moment—to love on a level beyond words, to help others as often as we can, and to find happiness in even the toughest times.

Chapter Three

Beyond NICU

To see my baby, I had to go through steel doors. I had to wash up to my elbows and sanitize as I had never done before. As the doors opened, I heard monitors beeping and saw boxes with babies in them, fighting for their lives.

How do you bond with a baby in a plastic box? How long would he be there? Why wasn't he crying? So many questions, so many fears. Graham did not utter a sound, and this felt so wrong to me. Where was his voice?

He began seizing on day seven. In comes the neurologist who earned the nickname "Dr. Doom and Gloom." He told us we had a 1% chance of having a normal baby. I felt hatred rage through my veins, as I looked at Greg. His shoulders were slumped, and his eyes were filled with tears. His pain and grief were visible. He was devastated by this statement. I watched his emotional breakdown. In the 17 years I had known him, I had never witnessed him lose it. I can still see his face and the pain on it.

Years later we discussed that doctor with another family—also a young couple that had never experienced hardship and were devastated by a difficult delivery. The doctor told these parents to unplug the respirator on the twin that had lived. Thank goodness they didn't listen, as she is still alive at age ten. Doctors have the power to empower parents to love and support their children no matter what. Sadly, too many out there are like Dr. Doom and Gloom.

In the NICU, Greg's coping mechanism was to watch the charts. Input and output, statistics...this was what he focused on. Somehow he could hold it together if he talked statistics with the doctors. I was different. I didn't care about the charts. I cared that my son wasn't crying. Not one sound. Why wasn't he making any sounds? When I asked the nurse, she stared into space. She eventually smiled sadly and walked away. There was no answer.

Then one day we heard it. A tiny cry coming from inside that plastic box. When sound came, it came with such force. He began to cry in NICU, and it didn't stop. When he was little it was not that loud—but you could hear the pain, and it didn't stop.

As he grew, he wailed in pain or agony. That tiny cry turned into a robust and loud cry. His cries pierced through us. It didn't stop. He cried every day for hours upon hours. He didn't sleep, could not console himself, and soon we were learning to accept this horrible sound. He had no control, and neither did we.

Graham could not turn the cries off. He cried every day, every hour, and we all lived through the torture of hearing him wail in agony. Way beyond colic, we were desperate to help him, searching endlessly for the doctor that could help us help him. I just wanted him to find inner peace.

I desperately wanted to end his pain and reduce his cries. He was four years old, and this was our existence...living with his pain and agony, listening to his cries day in and day out. None of us slept. Once a week Greg and I would take turns sleeping in the basement to get a full night's sleep so we could function.

Parents of newborns are sleep deprived the first few months. We were on our fourth year of sleepless nights and barely functioning. This was the beginning of feeling like Greg and I were on different planets—more than the guy/girl or Mars/Venus thing. Greg and I were emotionally in really different places.

Our marriage suffered. How could it not? We were both fighting to survive the stress, pain and grief of the situation.

We grew distant and talked mainly about the kids, mostly about Graham and his needs. I took on 80% of Graham's care while Greg took Colby and Tysen to sports practices or events that were difficult to manage with Graham.

I began to pull out of the emotional hell we both experienced before Greg did. I saw hope when he saw pain. In those days Greg hated to take Graham out in public. Greg used to be the guy who flew under the radar, he did not want attention. Those days were gone, and he resented the attention he was forced to endure because of Graham.

Chapter Four

Beyond the diagnoses

That first year was hell. Without a diagnosis, we didn't fit anywhere. We couldn't access information. We had no resources. We were essentially isolated from others. The local doctors had increased our burden through isolation.

When Graham was first born, one of my neighbors came over to tell me a difficult story of her first child, whom she lost at age one. The baby had a rare disease, and the memory of this was still painful to share with me. I was grateful that she would face her demons to help me. The man who helped her was a doctor in New York City, Arnold Gold. She suggested we see him. When I met him, we had an immediate connection.

He told me I reminded him of his wife. He was choked up as he gave us the news that our son had cerebral palsy, and he gently explained what this meant and what challenges may follow. He was kind in his manner.

He had a gentle disposition and even tried to defend the local doctors' care, offering that they chose their field in hopes of helping children—not hurting them. He acknowledged that the cavalier attitudes sometimes hurt the parents. This doctor was a true gentleman who regarded parents as valuable beings with feelings and took great care with how he interacted with us. Dr Gold gave me focus. I was now determined to focus on improving Graham's communication skills.

It was a day of acceptance. A day of grief. Confirmation of devastation... the diagnosis of cerebral palsy meant his life would be filled with difficulty and pain. Greg and I didn't speak in the elevator on the way out. As we hit the fresh air outside the building, the world looked different to me. I was coming from a darker place. I had no hope of a bright future. That is when we saw the old woman approach us.

She was a haggard woman who had been sitting on one of the benches that lined the sidewalks, her face wrinkled, clothes old and worn, a look of disgust carved into her face. She looked homeless, but I could not know that for sure. At first I looked at her and thought, *she has had a rough life. Let's put this in perspective. Graham has challenges to face, but he has us to help him and love him...and she is all alone. It could be worse.*

Then she looked into his eyes.

She was staring at the pavement and looked up at my son with a fleeting glance...and suddenly she appeared to melt in front of him. She completely transformed and was positively glowing inside and out after looking into his eyes. My mouth must have hung open. I looked down at this child with new eyes.

I suddenly saw that he was special in a way my eyes had never seen before. I could not see his reaction because he was in the stroller in front of us, but I wondered if he felt the connection or saw her change from pain to joy. I would be looking at him in the future in a completely different way, watching for these connections.

Who is he?

Why is he here?

He had reached her with no words, warmed her heart and left her a changed woman.

Then I shook it off and came to my senses. I put it aside like it had never happened.

But it did.

And I never forgot it.

My eyes opened that day. I did not look at my son and see what was wrong with him. I watched his effect on those who were open to receive him, and I learned what being open meant.

Chapter Five

Beyond stuck

How would we feed him? From the beginning it was tough, but we managed. He breastfed, with an adaptation. My nipple was too big for his tiny mouth (he was only 4lbs.), so I had to put a plastic nipple on to make it smaller—but it worked.

I remember one of the male doctors coming by and stopping dead in his tracks, staring at me feeding my son. "That's amazing! Oh—I'm sorry I don't mean to stare, but that is truly amazing!" At the moment it didn't matter that he was staring at my bare breast. I was proud of us. We found a way to do it.

It might have been more work, and it looked weird—but it worked. Talk about foreshadowing! More work, looking weird, and not caring would be a pattern with us in the future.

Graham was able to suck from a bottle, and so we transitioned from breastfeeding to bottle feeding. He could not hold the bottle himself or feed himself, so one of us was always helping him. One Christmas we took a picture of my son holding his own bottle with both hands.

He was in his great grandmother's arms, and she excitedly said "OH! Look! Look what he's doing!" He was two years old. It was at Christmas, and in my family scrapbook page the caption reads: "Christmas Magic." While he never would be able to feed himself independently, we did not know that yet. In that moment Graham had magically presented hope that he might.

One day I tried to give my son milk out of a cup, and he surprised both of us by drinking it! I was so excited. It was more work, and it looked different, but he did it. Greg wasn't too excited about more work and stuck with bottles, until one day I threw them all out.

"He's ready Dad, so you have to move on with him. No holding him back because it's easier on us." It wasn't easy for him to feed Graham, he got frustrated with the process. So, I began feeding him 80% of the time. It was easier on all of us.

Let's talk formula. I breastfed for three months, and then my doctor suggested it was too stressful for me. With tremendous guilt that I was putting myself first, I stopped. My first son nursed for fourteen months. My second, for ten.

Three months seemed like giving up to me. After he stopped nursing, he started throwing up white stuff. Reflux, they thought. The first gastrointestinal doctor made us wait in the waiting room for an hour and a half with a screaming baby, and then she said in a cavalier way, "Put a g-tube in him." That meant surgery to place a tube into his stomach, and he would not eat with his mouth. We refused. I told the doctor, "He can eat. We will find another way."

First we tried a soy formula, but he had an allergic reaction and vomited violently. Then we tried something called Nutramigen. We had to buy it from the pharmacy, and it smelled disgusting. What was I feeding him?

My dad offered to pick up a case for us until he heard it was over $500! Next, we took him to a specialist who did the pH-probe to test for reflux. A pH-probe is when they put a tube in your child's nose down his throat and measure what happens when you feed him acidic juices. It was terrible to watch when he reacted in pain after having the juice, but it came up empty.

The doctor suggested a drug called Reglan, which she warned had a side effect of causing seizures. Greg and I exchanged a look, and I knew exactly what he was thinking:

Are you insane? You want us to give a child prone to seizures a medicine that can cause seizures?

Needless to say, we found another doctor. This one disregarded the pH-probe results and said, "Let's try him on the reflux meds. There is no downside." And guess what? It helped. It significantly reduced the frequency of his vomiting. You name it, he's thrown up there. On himself, on us, his bed, the table, the car, at dinner, a movie.

One time he threw up on the person in front of him at a Broadway show. That was a proud moment. Glad it was Dad with him that time. Another memory: just as we were served our appetizers at a fancy restaurant, he threw up all over the food. The staff quickly changed the cloth, brought new food, and we all kept eating like nothing had happened.

I got to be an expert on the grab-and-turn. Grab him, turn him over on his belly and help him get it out. His tone makes him arch his back, which makes it hard to vomit, and he could choke on it. What's trying to come up and out falls back into his throat. It's frightening if he is strapped into his wheelchair when this happens. He is so strong, it is difficult to unstrap him and turn him.

Worse yet, it's terrifying to wake up in the night and hear him choking. Imagine turning on the light and finding vomit in his eyes, hair, nose, mouth: it was everywhere. His sounds were muffled by vomit, but as we cleared that away, the very scared cry emerged.

He cannot roll over or clear the vomit himself. I wondered what he thought, what he felt, but there was no way to know for sure. It had happened several times. I heard him every time and was able to get there to help him.

My worst experience with vomit ever was at a 95th birthday celebration for his great grandmother in Washington D.C. It was 2008.

Unbeknownst to us, he had been fed expired milk at school accidently. We were in a hotel in D.C. for the family celebration. He vomited so many times, I slept on the floor next to his mattress, too afraid it would happen while he was sleeping. It did.

I was groggy, a little slow on the grab-and-turn, and he vomited into my mouth and in my hair. My husband came running and grabbed him as I ran to the shower, tears streaming down my face. I didn't want to move from the shower. I couldn't move.

My husband gently helped me out and put me into bed with one of the older boys. I slept in the fetal position and cried myself to sleep. The next day we had to pretend everything was fine and attend the birthday celebration. Things were not fine.

What about feeding? Well, a long time ago my therapist told me I fed Graham in and "unorthodox" way. I fed him way too much, and way too fast, but it worked for him so I didn't care.

He warned me that no therapist with feeding training would feel comfortable feeding him so much, so fast. I never dreamed that it would go on for years but at ten, I would still see it. The therapists' fear I mean. They all worried about him aspirating or choking and so the feeding difficulties would continue.

For various reasons, when Graham was almost two years old we were just starting to introduce solid foods. He had to learn how to swallow and use his tongue to push food back into his mouth. The process was slow.

Soon we started pureed food. When he cut teeth, his bottom tooth severed his tongue during a tonal spasm, and he looks like he has a serpent tongue to this day. (A tonal spasm is when Graham's body contorts and twists and he cannot control it.) Well, that ended that, no more pureed food, and he was back to formula.

The new one: PediaSure. He would only drink the vanilla. He spit up every other flavor. He would projectile vomit white liquid, which I later learned was chyme, undigested material from inside his body.

Tonal spasms are a part of Graham. They fluctuated through the years, sometimes frequent, and sometimes not. They did not always look the same. His arms might stiffen, or his head might turn to the right. We would learn to accept that this was part of who he was. How many years would this go on?

Chapter Six

Beyond play

How do I play with my child? This child is different. I already had two children and am the type of mom who dresses up as Superman with her kids, cape and all! I was caught by a UPS man in my own backyard in my cape, and while a bit embarrassed, I would do it again in a heartbeat.

I would have done anything for my kids! But this child could not use his hands, and he could not talk. Contrary to what seems natural, we did everything in our power not to make him laugh. Why? Because he would throw up violently after laughing. So how, then, could I play with him?

The natural tendency for us as humans is to make a baby smile or laugh. Each time someone tried this with Graham, I would have to distract him in hopes that he did not vomit. I had to ask people not to make him laugh. Those who didn't listen felt awful after they made him laugh and he vomited.

I stared at toys he could never use. He could not hold a ball or a stuffed animal. He could not play games. I watched his older brothers play while he watched. Is this how it would be? Almost like watching everyone else do something and being on the outside of a glass door, unable to take part?

Not on my watch. I would find a way to include him. It hurt too much to see him isolated. We did puppet shows, and we made up stories about stuffed animals. One day Graham's older brother, Tysen, grew out of his tricycle and insisted I save it for Graham. I couldn't tell him his brother would never ride his beloved bike. He didn't see his brother as "different" yet, and I wasn't going to be the one to force him there.

There were so many heartaches like this. It seemed like the world turned into a place that he didn't fit in. We saw all the things he couldn't ever do.

You name it, I bought it—thinking maybe he could do this or that. Playing became playing by myself to make him laugh—not playing with him. The house was filled with giant coloring books he'd never color, books he could not read, games we tried to include him in. I've always wanted him to be able to play independently.

I tried books on tape, view master movies, interactive DVD games, computer games...and none of it worked. He would sit with you, content to watch.

When he was older, about 10, he would play Peek-a-Boo with my Dad, who had Alzheimer's. The game is for small children or babies, and Graham was much too old for it, but he knew his response would make my Dad happy...so he did it for him. Amazing.

The third child has to do what the older kids or parents drag them to a lot. Many third children get toted around, but this was different. Imagine never being able to choose what you want to do. Always doing what someone else chooses. Sitting alone. Not being able to say a word. Watching the world in silence. I tried not to think about it. It's too painful. He was trapped in a body with no voice.

Beyond being alone: So is it okay to leave Graham alone? On the one hand, I could not imagine having someone with me all day long, as Graham has always had to endure. Think about this for a minute. How often are you alone?

What if someone was always with you? Graham needs help with all daily living skills, so he cannot be alone...and yet I wondered if he had enough space to just be.

The flip side to that is that if he is never alone because I am always with him...then I too am never alone. I didn't realize how much that had affected me. I had lost the sense of myself. Did he have a sense of himself? Was he lonely?

We got a television that hangs from the ceiling as a test to see if he could watch by himself. Success. It was the first time he could just be alone, content and at peace. What a huge difference it made. It was the best summer ever! We watched cartoons, educational shows, mysteries...you name it!

As he got older he wanted to spend more and more time alone watching TV in his bedroom. He was safe, content and independent. So why did I feel guilty?

Was I ignoring him? Not paying enough attention? Unclear. It wasn't like he could tell me. (Later, when he could tell me with eye gaze technology, he confirmed that he likes his down time just like the rest of us.)

I felt uneasy. I walked the dogs for ten minutes in my neighborhood, and the whole time Graham was on my mind. He was happily in his bed watching football when I returned. "He is a teenager, Mom. He can be alone," said Tysen. There is truth to that. However, I still felt guilty leaving him for 10 minutes to walk my dog outside, and that was my reality, my truth.

We began the journey into modified play. Watching a stranger play with my son with a button called a switch. You touch or hit the button and something happens (cause and effect). Graham was disinterested.

His teacher or therapist would ask me what he likes, and I would look at them and think, *Are you insane? How would I know? He doesn't seem to like anything.*

Instead I would smile and say, "Nothing in particular yet" with a knot in my stomach. Watching TV and videos were all I could do with him. I knew he watched them, and he was content.

How did I know? He did not cry, he quietly watched. Great, content. Not exactly playing happily. Did he even like it? I had no idea. Until one day...

Bear in the Big Blue House came on. He was three years old, sitting in his chair watching TV like my other boys did...but it wasn't the same. He just sat there. He didn't interact, move or make a sound. I was upstairs getting laundry done while he was quiet, and suddenly I heard Graham making an unfamiliar sound.

My heart beating fast, I ran to the stairs to look over the banister and make sure he wasn't throwing up or choking...and I saw it. A great big smile. Then laughter. He was wildly giggling.

I literally stopped, rubbed my eyes in disbelief and waited. Bear sniffed the screen (his nose got very big with a silly sound), and there it was again. The cutest giggle I thought I'd ever heard. We had found something he liked!

Disney had a Play House Disney Show. We took him to it, and the magic of Disney was there as he watched in awe as he saw Bear in person! We bought t-shirts, stuffed animals, books, whatever we could find to make him happy. His personality showed itself, and now that I had seen him happy I was on a mission to make it happen whenever and however I could.

Barney was next. I had tons of videos from my older boys. We watched them all. We took Graham to Universal Studios to the Barney Show when he was four to meet Barney in person! I had tears in my eyes, looking at the wonder in his eyes as he smiled for a picture with the gigantic purple dinosaur.

Elmo was the next favorite. Tickle me Elmo, Elmo's World, a personalized Elmo that says, "Graham, will you be my Valentine?" Off to Sesame Place in New Jersey for more smiles and a private picture with Elmo. Graham was five.

For his birthday his nanny dressed up in an Elmo costume and came to our house with balloons for him. Elmo pulled a wagon that Graham laid in to the swing set and took him swinging. He was wide-eyed and full of smiles. Whatever we could to do make him feel special, we did.

Disney did it best. The staff was kind to us, helping us to use the wheelchair tie downs. Up until that point we did not want to make people wait and would take Graham out of the stroller and hold him and the equipment. The staff gently helped us to realize this was not the best way for him or for us.

The Disney staff really knew how to make people feel special. I would take Graham to the shows while the older boys rode the roller coasters with Dad. The Little Mermaid, Beauty and the Beast, the Lion King, Tarzan; he loved them all. Smiling and squealing with delight during the shows, Graham enjoyed it all. The singers and dancers always had a special smile or wink for the children in the handicapped section. It was heart-warming to feel other people make an extra effort to get my son to smile.

As he aged, there were new favorites: The Incredibles, SpongeBob SquarePants, Shrek, Cars, Wall-E and Monsters Inc. were next on the list. We kept visiting the parks to fill his life with special memories, his room with pictures of Graham with his favorite characters.

When the Toy Story 3D movie came out, Greg and I smiled through the entire movie, watching Graham grinning and laughing louder than anyone there. He just loved it, and watching his pure joy is a gift.

 He has an infectious smile, and he gets everyone around him to smile or laugh with him when he is happy. The light he brings to the world has brightened so many lives.

Chapter Seven

Beyond words

What if your child could not hug you or call you by name? Every day when Colby and Tysen got up and ready for school there were lots of hugs and kisses. Our favorite saying was "I hope you have a happy day."

It stung when I would look at Graham and think that I would to never hear the words "I love you" or get hugs and kisses from him. How would you feel if you never got a hug or kiss from your little one?

The ache in my heart seemed so deep. Maybe it wouldn't have hurt as much if I didn't have two children already. I had experienced their first words, the "I love you, Mommy" and the joy of hearing whatever came out of their sweet little mouths as they learned about their world.

Colby saying "lellow" instead of yellow and "pliglet" instead of piglet. The adorable voice I can still hear. Would I ever hear "I love you" from Graham? Could he ever express love? Would he physically be able to hug me?

I remember feeling so hurt by another mom who had a child with special needs when Graham was at his preschool. I had just picked Graham up and was headed toward my car in the parking lot when this other mom declared she just didn't know how she would ever live through this autism thing if her son couldn't tell her he loved her...everything stopped for me. *What? Did she really just say that?*

It felt as if the wind got knocked out of me. My child was nonverbal, and she knew I would never hear those words from his mouth. How could she be so insensitive? How could I be hurt by someone who was supposed to get it?

Her child proceeded to come running to the car, and in his tiny little voice said, "I love you, Mommy," wrapping his arms around her. I turned toward my car as the tears rolled down my cheeks. The reality of my situation consumed me.

I drove home with an overwhelmingly painful knowing in my heart that I would never hear my little boy say those words to me. Years later I know that this mother had no idea she was hurting me. I had accepted that Graham did not use words, and I grieved the loss.

Would he ever be able to kiss me? Most likely the answer is no. Somewhere over the years Graham learned his version of a kissing sound...but that's as close as I will ever get to his kiss, I think. Oh well. It wouldn't stop me from bestowing him with tons of kisses.

I had to accept many things I could not control. Hugs, kisses, a long list of other things he could not do. The only thing that kept me going was Graham. His smile, his laugh, his love. If there is one thing I am sure of, it's that Graham knows he is loved. He probably feels more loved than most typical children.

I know he felt more loved than I did when I was growing up. I was the baby by nine years, and by that time it was a busy house, and I got dragged along to whatever was going on with the family.

While Graham got dragged everywhere too, it was different. He was the center of our world...or we were in Graham's world, and he was showing us countless things we had never known before.

Because of Graham we try harder, forgive sooner, give further, thank easier, hope longer, love deeper and laugh louder.

"How old is he?"

I hated that question. Some days I was ready to smile, give his age and ignore the reaction. But most days? I got a lump in my stomach and would bite out the words, turning my son away so he wouldn't be hurt by their surprise. He was very small and looked like a toddler. "He weighs 39 pounds, and he is 10 years old."

It used to be worse. When he was five years old people would ask, "How old is the baby?" and I would inwardly cringe and smile as I told them his age.

Like I said, I hate that question. It focuses on how different he looks. Most days I was grateful for his size. By the time he was eight years old, I had already thrown my back out lifting him. I stopped playing golf immediately without a second thought. I went to a trainer to make sure I was in physical shape to care for my son.

Chapter Eight

Beyond normal

We tried to keep things normal in our lives. What is normal really? Could things ever be normal? Were things ever normal? What was my definition of normal? Like many things, I would redefine what I thought about normal. For now, it meant that we did all we could to keep up with the boys' activities and Graham's therapies. We could barely handle that, let alone keep a social life. We hardly saw anyone.

We have lived our lives and included him in as much as we could. In fact, we had to learn that it was okay not to include him. We fought so fiercely to be his advocates and include him in all parts of our lives that we couldn't see that separation is good for all parents and children. It was a hard lesson to learn.

We have traveled far and wide with Graham: St. Lucia, Bahamas, California, Arizona, Nevada, Washington D.C., Florida, Massachusetts, New York City, Disney World—even a Disney Cruise.

So many of us are so busy in our lives that we don't notice the nuance of the situation. Our family felt his effect on people, and we were grateful for his gift. Even the older boys would notice how Graham would affect strangers in an airport, crowded place, or restaurant: they could see the person connect with Graham and smile, and appreciate that as a gift.

Graham and I faced my fear of heights together, wheeling right up to the edge, just the two of us, at the Grand Canyon. It was a serene, profound moment. I thanked Graham out loud for helping me to face so many fears. I told him how proud I was of us and that I knew we'd have many more adventures together.

He smiled with his whole body: raised his shoulders, arched his back, and grinned from ear to ear. Once you've seen that smile you know what I mean and somehow feel it throughout your own body as well.

We took Graham to Yosemite National Park. It had snowed, so not all of the paths were clear. It didn't stop us. We lifted his wheelchair over the debris so he could see the redwood trees with us. We went until the path had stairs, and then Graham and I waited while the boys went on to see a bigger tree called the old Sequoia. The picture of Greg and I lifting Graham is etched in my mind. No physical barrier would stop him if we could help it!

We tried it all. Greg took Colby, Tysen, and Graham golfing. Graham at first was in a car seat in the golf cart. I was scared he would get hit with a ball. I thought he might be bored going. I thought Greg would be embarrassed to take him. When I asked if Greg was sure he said, "Just let anyone try to stop me."

This turned out to be one of Greg's steps in accepting our situation and who Graham was. He wanted to golf with his sons. All of them. Later, he used a jogging stroller to run with him as Graham got bigger.

Greg used to bike and run with Graham. He would take him on the Sea Doo (jet-ski) and spin in circles as fast as he does with the other boys, while I would have a heart attack on shore, thinking of how Graham couldn't swim if he fell in. Greg would often take him on a long boat ride, just the two of them.

We had an adapted bike that strapped Graham on the front of Greg's bike and attracted a lot of attention as we biked on the Erie Canal one year. It was Father's Day, and we had a picnic and tried out the new bike. Later, we got him a bike he could use himself.

A substitute therapist asked if she could use it with him at school during the winter, and we were thrilled. What a great way for him to use his muscles! I got a call the day I dropped it off at the school saying I had to come pick it up again.

"Why?"

"We can't use equipment from home," they told me. What? Musical instruments and calculators were from home. Where is this coming from?

"If Graham gets to bring his bike to school then all students should be able to bring their bikes to school". That's insane. Graham has to be strapped into his bike. It's a therapy bike. Where was this coming from? Who would do this to him? The Director of Special Education.

We had to call the Superintendent of our school district to get her to look into this ridiculous situation. We were ready to mount a petition and fight to let Graham ride his bike at school if it was needed. We soon got a phone call inviting Graham to use his bike at school. Turns out our fight with the school district would be later.

Being in public

In the beginning it seemed like Greg had a hard time being in public with Graham. Graham cried non-stop and had floppy tone. We were met with comments like "He's tired," and "Looks like a sack of potatoes you're carrying," and "Can't keep his eyes open huh?"

At times we would quip back, "No, he can't hold his head up because he has cerebral palsy. He's not tired." Sometimes we got looks of sympathy or apologies when they heard our response. Sometimes they just stared. It got easier for us to ignore it as time went on.

I hated the car rides, as Graham's crying pierced my heart—and it broke repeatedly as I drove Tysen to preschool, went home, then picked him up and drove home again: four times daily, all to blood curdling scream cries, five days a week.

Greg somehow could handle the car rides better than I could. He found a way to ignore or accept it that I could not. But he didn't do it four times a day, five days a week, like I did. So when he did drive, he had more tolerance.

Even going to the movies was difficult and painful. It is unbelievable how many people without disabilities sit in the accessible seating area. We would ask people to leave and they would be rude to us. It was bad enough we had to sit there but to have to fight to sit there?

Then one time I will never forget. I heard Graham making the sound he makes when he poops and closed my eyes thinking please not now... little could I have imagined that he would have a blow out right there in the movie theater.

There was diarrhea on the floor under his wheel chair and it stunk. I had paper towels I threw on the carpet to cover it, Greg and I wheeled him out to the family bathroom to change him but we had no spare clothes so I had to run to the store and buy some. Good thing we were in the mall. I could never have handled this on my own. Now going to the movies is scary to me.

I wouldn't go to Wegman's to shop for groceries unless I had a sitter. I always ended up in tears if I tried to bring Graham with me. The therapists would suggest taking a trip to Wegman's as an outing or adventure. They had no idea how bad it was. It was torture to me and not fair to Graham. He hated it too.

Ten years later I still prefer to shop on my own, but Dad braves Wegman's with Graham a lot. He says, "It's fun because it's as if the seas are parting"—meaning people can't get out of the way of Graham's wheelchair quickly enough. Funny how your perspective changes.

In his younger years Greg dreaded taking Graham to events and would do anything to avoid it. I clung to my mama bear protective mantra: he can do anything anyone else can. I would ignore the stares and teach people there were different ways of doing things by leading through example. "God Bless You" and "You are wonderful with him" would follow as together we faced each new situation. It didn't mean I didn't hate it.

Beyond the stares:

On display yet again...

There are days when you wish you could fade away...

not us,

not ever again.

Chapter Nine

Beyond toilet training

Who would have thought I'd be changing diapers for twenty years straight? Usually a child gets potty trained at two to four years old. Usually. There is nothing usual about parenting a child with special needs. My child was fully dependent for his personal care needs. That meant eating, toileting, bathing...you get the drift.

I was not a nurse. My husband and I had no medical training. What we have learned to do is astounding. I remember changing my first child's poopy diaper. It was almost exciting that this little human being was doing new things, and at that point poop was maybe a teaspoon full of wet discolored material that hardly resembled what we think of as poop.

Then there were the days when Tysen, child #2, decided he was going to poop wherever he wanted to. The bathtub, the carpet... I had to find a way to gather the strength to clean it up and teach him right from wrong with patience and love, all while trying to control my anger or frustration. Exactly how would I do that with Graham?

Potty training a child who could not sit without assistance. Could it be done? The search began. Catalogs revealed equipment I could strap him into: basically a commode. We didn't know if he would be able to do it, but off we were on to the next hurdle.

His bladder was so small at 35 pounds that he was going every half hour and our backs were paying the price: for Graham to go to the bathroom on an adapted toilet seat I needed to (1) lift him to the changing table to undress him, (2) lift and bring him to the toilet, (3) lift him to wipe, (4) lift and bring him back to the changing table, (5) dress him and lift him back into his chair.

Graham's bladder was so small he had to go to the bathroom every 30-45 minutes. That meant all that lifting every 30-45 minutes, all day long. We could not support this, and toilet training was put on hold. I had tremendous guilt about that.

This was not going to work. School could not support it at every half hour, so we had to compromise to change him four times a day at school unless he "told us" he was uncomfortable and needed a change. It's one of those things you are asked to accept that is hard to do.

We tried pull-ups to teach him what wetting through felt like, which added quite a few changes in the beginning. He got it but could never hold it longer than thirty minutes. It was a heartbreaking decision to put him back in diapers because we could not physically support him until he grew bigger and could hold it longer. It had to be done.

I had tremendous guilt that I'd given him independence and taken it away. What if he couldn't do it again and Graham was faced with a lifelong dependency on diapers because I couldn't physically handle it? It wasn't just me— school couldn't support it either—but I ached inside. We moms have a way of feeling guilty about everything.

When he was 40 pounds and growing out of size 6 diapers—the biggest size diapers come in—I panicked. I wasn't sure what to do next. Networking with other parents is how I figured it out. You would think one of the many doctor's offices we visited would help us with personal care issues...but that was not our experience. Nope.

What would we do when he grew out of diapers? What did other people do? How did big kids or adult's toilet? Is there a store for this stuff? There are medical supply companies that can help, and we now have our supplies delivered to the house. It would have been great if someone had told us years earlier.

As he grew bigger, how would I change him? I used to pick him up by holding both feet, suspending him while I wiped his bottom. Now that he was bigger I had to learn to roll him on his side. It took pulling the muscles in my back to get me to realize that I could no longer lift him this way. It was difficult to accept my own limitations.

When he hit 55 pounds, I could no longer lift Graham. I needed a mechanical lift to help me. The world still expects families to lift their children. Every doctor's office I go to expects us to pick Graham up out of the wheelchair and weigh him while holding him. That was fine when he was 35 pounds. Now, not so much.

Greg can still lift him and does, and he will push until he hurts himself. The medical community should be helping families learn to navigate a world like this and provide support, but that is not the case (yet). It's about dignity for the client as well as protecting families and staff from injury.

Toileting is a fact of life. One we take for granted—and most of us don't realize how lucky we are to go to the bathroom whenever we want to. What would it be like to wear diapers or Depends and rely on other people to change you your entire life?

How would Graham toilet at school? On a field trip? At the mall? At a restaurant? On a plane? I could not ask him how he felt. He did not know any different, and we could not change his situation for him...so why ask?

When he was small enough we could use the baby changing stations in public rest rooms. I remember my husband's story of when one of those plastic stations broke while Graham was on it because he was too heavy.

Thankfully my husband was strong enough to keep him from falling to the ground, and somehow he managed to finish the job and get him back in his wheelchair, safe and clean.

What would I have done? What did I do when driving on a trip and he had a blowout? I asked his older brother Colby to carry him into the ladies' room and put him on the fold out table for me. Colby was embarrassed to be in the ladies' room. "Mom, you have to tell people I am going in there before we go in," he said.

Okay, here goes: "My son has to come with me into the ladies' room because I cannot hold my other son to change him." I was desperate. Graham was covered in poop—it was on his chair, it was everywhere.

As soon as he could, Colby ran out of that ladies' room and waited outside until I needed him. I asked someone to tell Colby to come in and get Graham. As he wheeled him out, he accidently brought the blue changing pad covered in poop with him. Now it was all over the floor outside the bathroom.

I was still cleaning up inside and had no idea what was happening outside. A kind-hearted employee got paper towels and a mop and helped Colby clean up. In that dark moment, the kindness shown by a stranger pulled us through. We were ashamed, embarrassed, hating that things like this happen to our family...but grateful for the kindness of a stranger. In that moment we could focus on the good in that person, and how she helped us without being asked.

Airplane toileting?

Traveling has become a toileting nightmare for us. At age ten, while he was small, Graham was not small enough to fit on a baby changing table anymore. He could not stand on his own or sit on his own. Some airline personnel were empathetic, trying to help however they could.

Others refused to let us put him on the galley floor on a blanket to change him. I vividly remember asking one woman through my tears what she wanted me to do, and her hardened response, "You cannot change him there," as she walked away. She left us no choice, and feeling like I was doing something wrong, I quickly changed him on a blanket on my lap, crying and apologizing to those nearby, faintly saying I didn't know what else to do.

Several "God bless you's" and "I can't believe how mean she was" settled me for a bit. I just held him tight. What would I do now? Why was the world so cruel? What would our future be like? Does no one else travel? Are we back in the dark ages where people with disabilities should not be seen or fly on planes?

We were not giving up. We kept flying. Two of us with an open door was our next attempt. Privacy gone, out the window, we tried to be as fast as we could. One sat on the closed toilet seat and held Graham up as best she/he could.

 It is no easy task to hold someone up who cannot stand on their own. The other, on hands and knees, pulls down the pants, takes the diaper off, tries to cover him while cleaning him and ignoring the stares. If you get a nice attendant they might hold a blanket up.

I'll always remember the one attendant that yelled at my husband for blocking the aisle and stood over him, yelling at him to go back to his seat. He was so angered by her that he forgot us, stood up, and started to yell back. I frantically tried to get his attention back, as my naked child was stripped of all dignity.

There are times, such as this one, when we snap. We sat in shame for the remainder of the flight, taking turns holding Graham tightly and telling him how much we love him.

Airplane seats—another challenge. When he could fit in a car seat we had a bit of a rest, although he preferred to be held. As he grew, we would have to hold him up in his seat propped with pillows for takeoff and landing.

The twist of your back for 30-40 minutes was hard, not to mention his crying. He didn't want to be in his seat, and everyone on the plane knew it. The four-hour flights were brutal and emotional hell.

Some parents don't try to stop the child from crying on an airplane. We tried everything we could think of but still could not stop his cries. We sang to him, we rocked him, we read to him, we talked to him, we passed him to each other and to his brothers, and nothing worked.

We traveled every year. We rarely saw any other children with disabilities flying. Finally, when Graham was ten years old, they came out with a five point harness seatbelt for plane travel that supported him independently.

Secure and comfortable at last, he flew for two straight hours and never moved. I didn't hold him, need to entertain him, nothing. Finally, I had a break. I did nothing that whole flight, and I was in heaven.

Chapter Ten

Beyond hearing

I remember when the staff at the Ear Nose and Throat (ENT) doctor's office told us Graham was deaf. He was a year old. He would need hearing aids for the rest of his life. I watched the videotape the staff sent us home with him, crying in disbelief. How could he not hear us? We had so many tests done. Some sedated, some behavioral, all pointing to hearing loss. Moderate to severe hearing loss. Breathe.

I didn't know anyone who is deaf. I had never seen a hearing aid before. How do they work? Like a microphone for your ear. You can have one that hangs on your neck or one that is a BTE, behind the ear. Which part do you put in the ear? Well, each person has an ear mold made for the ear that needs amplification.

An audiologist squirts a foamy substance in your ear canal and lets it harden, similar to orthodontic impressions of your teeth. It is sent away and a soft plastic mold with a clear tube attached comes back, which attaches to the BTE. You will need to clean the wax out of the hearing aids several times daily. Yuck. Ear wax was now a part of my life.

The audiologists told us Graham was deaf when he was two. Not totally deaf, but hearing impaired. After multiple attempts at hearing tests locally we were told he needed sedated testing to measure the amount of hearing loss.

We took Graham to Massachusetts Eye and Ear for a sedated ABR. This place has more information on lower tones. We found out a lot. Graham's loss is moderate in both ears. His loss was in the low and high tones but he was not amplified in the low tones for two years. His aids are too powerful for his loss. He was over amplified. We need new aids.

We were told he had a bilateral moderate loss and would need to wear hearing aids in both ears. We took him for a second opinion. We all learned sign language, and it was amazing to watch him respond. His hearing loss was the first concrete answer we had that confirmed a disability. We joked that we learned "baby sign." The boys had to pick sign names, and it was cute watching what they came up with.

The first hearing aids we had made were tan. After losing them in the grass several times, we switched to bright colors. Our family still laughs about the time we lost a hearing aid in the grass and my two and a half year old said, "Oh, the skunk probably took it" rather matter-of-factly. (None of us had ever seen a skunk near our house, so we're not quite sure where that came from, but he seemed pretty sure.)

So we chose bright blue for the next hearing aids, thinking it would be much easier to find. In the course of ten years the dog ate one, we vacuumed one by mistake, ran over one...you name it, we've done it! As Graham got older he made his own color choices—orange and blue (the colors of Syracuse University) and finally camouflage in middle school. We began to see his personality emerge.

Greg, the kids, the sitter and I took sign language—or at least "baby sign," as I call it. We spent months with a therapist learning to sign. The alphabet, name signs, yes/no for the kids was it. We learned holidays, loud/soft, toilet, play, etc.

I never quite got the hang of reading it or using conversational sign language, and I was grateful that—with his aids on—he could rely on his hearing. He soon made it clear he did not need sign language and reliably reacted to auditory input.

At this point I'm feeling alone. I'm doing occupational therapy, physical therapy, speech therapy and signing. I'm working on feeding techniques. My sitters are helping with feeding but no one seems to be signing but me and as it is I'm such a beginner I'm not doing a good enough job. It's like everyone feels his hearing aids will magically make things better. There is so much work to be done and I cannot do it all myself. I'm not quite sure what to do about it yet.

I tried to sign to someone else years ago during a Hyperbaric Oxygen (HBOT) tank dive. Oxygen treatment is used in hospitals to rehabilitate burn victims, scuba divers and other people with acute conditions. Now HBOT is available to the private sector.

I had practiced all night so I could sign two words (beautiful girl) to this young girl. The mother criticized me immediately, and in a disapproving tone told her daughter I didn't mean to call her a fat girl. I was crushed—apologizing, but not understanding what I had done wrong.

She then explained that there were two languages: American Sign Language and Signed English—and there was a lot of controversy within the deaf community over which was used. The girl's mother did not recognize the other language, which was the one I stayed up all night learning.

She refused to use it and was therefore not accepting what I had said to her daughter. I had no idea there was more than one or that there was controversy about which one to use.

I thought to myself that I would have been thrilled that someone tried to communicate with my child, not yelling at them for using the "other language."

It was 2006. I was on the down part of the rollercoaster. Fighting the school for services. Everyone told me it would only get worse. Lots of parents gave up because it was too hard to fight. We kept thinking that if we were reasonable they would listen. We had no idea how unreasonable they would be.

I realized that at his school they talked about him, in front of him, over him...but not to him. We tried to learn the appropriate process. We followed the rules and we were met with denial of services, negative attitudes and disrespect and it made no sense at all. There is always a way to disagree respectfully. We understood the school could not do everything for every student but this was a battle about control and ego and not our child's needs.

Parents think that a school helping their child is just going to happen automatically (a given). What about the day you realize it's not happening? I have seen so many parents crushed as they realize the basic premise we all believe, that everyone wants to help our children at school, is not always the case.

In the world of special education there are meetings, legal papers that say one thing but the staff sometimes does another. The law says you have to do this for my child, but the reality is that it doesn't always happen—and the parents have to fight to get it done. How far will you take it?

Many give up. Others sell their houses and move to other districts. Some will take legal action. All of us hate that we are in the fight at all. It shouldn't be this way. They should want what's best for my child.

Chapter Eleven

Beyond birthdays

How do you celebrate a day that brought such pain? You pretend to be happy celebrating the birthday for your other children and cry behind closed doors. We would have cake, even though he couldn't eat it. We would have a party and a theme, because that's what we did with the older boys. Preschool was Elmo, then Barney, then Cars and SpongeBob.

Graham's first few birthdays were just family. When he began preschool, we brought the party to the classroom, and the family came too. Party hats, decorations, goodie bags—we tried to make it a special celebration for everyone. We had a cowboy party at the adaptive riding program and brought the whole preschool to the event. When he was in kindergarten we tried bowling.

I'll never forget the pain I felt when he was in first grade. Graham didn't have any friends to ask to a birthday party. He didn't have any friends at all. So his school party was all I had planned to do. I remember crying and walking the aisles of the stores, searching for something that would truly be for him.

I couldn't bring food he couldn't eat (cupcakes or cookie cake were what my older boys wanted at his age) or toys he couldn't play with. That might have worked when he was younger, but he was old enough to understand now.

I settled on smiley stickers and lollipops that he could pass out. That would be his kid celebration. I drove to his school and was early and very nervous. I was trying to be happy, to accept that different is not always bad and that celebrating just at school would be okay.

I came with my camera, but I was early... so they asked me to come back. I went to get coffee. When I came back in, it was over. I saw that all the kids had their stuff. I saw Graham sitting in the room of peers with a blank look on his face. I felt stupid holding the camera when there was nothing to take a picture of.

They had done it without me and taken his birthday away from me. I barely held my tears until I hit the front door of the school and cried all the way home. I had been trying to accept that he didn't have to have a party with kids—that we could celebrate in a different way. And they stole that from me. I felt hurt, betrayed, and angry.

Today I understand that they did not know this hurt. I hope that they read this and know it now so that other mothers are spared that pain.

At the time, I was chairing the Ice Cream Social event for the school. I called the vendor I rented the jumpy houses from and ordered a gigantic castle. I told him the story and said I wanted Graham to see it from the bus when he got home and vowed that I would make his birthday special despite what had happened at school.

I called my nanny and asked her to dress as Elmo and bring him balloons. Elmo took him swinging, took him in the bouncy house, and pulled him in his wagon. I cried. The man left the bouncy house for four days and would not let me pay. He said it was the least he could do to try and ease my pain.

We sent a thank you note from my son, and he called to tell me what it meant to him. My answer to him was this: "When someone goes out of their way to show kindness when the world can be so cruel, it's important to recognize it."

Would Graham ever be asked to someone else's birthday party? It hurt to hope. It hurt to think about my sweet little boy being left out. Graham heard other kids talking about birthday parties, and I think he knew he was not invited...but he could not tell me if this hurt his feelings. I was hurt for him. I tried not to think about it and then one day an invitation came.

Graham was invited to a birthday party! I was thrilled. I didn't know if anyone would ever include him in what seems like a typical part of a child's life. I was excited and so was Graham. Of course he could just be reacting to my excitement, we would not know until the party.

The first one was from another boy with disabilities. His disabilities were not as severe as Graham's, so even there we felt out of place, and a lot of relatives attending would stare or say things they didn't know were hurtful. "What's wrong with him?" Heavy sigh. *What's wrong with you?* I would silently retort. Graham kept a straight face. I could not ask him if it hurt.

The next year it was a backyard Olympics party. I sent my husband, knowing I could not physically support Graham if we attempted to include him in the festivities, doubtful that many things would be possible. He told me he never wanted to do that again. He had just experienced being the only parent participating in the kids' activities.

He was on display with a great big dose of seeing your child as not belonging that I felt at these things. Would it have been better not to take him to the parties? It might have been easier on us, but this was about Graham.

Next was a karate party where I was the only mom out there with the kids because I had to hold Graham up in the circle. He couldn't sit by himself. All the other parents sat in the waiting area. I felt stupid and on display as I tried to attempt some of the activities. It was so uncomfortable.

I got smarter later and asked my sitter to come to the parties to help me. Good thing, because the next party was a pool party—an above ground pool with 15 kids and no adults in it. I tried to explain to the birthday girl why I couldn't put Graham in the pool with all of the kids.

I explained to Graham why he could not go in the pool. Did that bother him? Did he want to go in? I don't know. We tried to help him participate. The sitter and I held him up to the side so he could toss a beach ball to the kids in the pool and be part of it in some way.

He was so heavy we had to take turns, and we were both sweating after a half hour. They served pizza. He can't eat pizza. He could only drink, so we gave him his Ensure, and they all stared as he drank it. He looked serious. It did not seem like he was having fun anymore. I know I wasn't having fun anymore.

He had been asked to one birthday party a year. The last one was a sledding party. Again, I was the only parent there and had to sit and be a part of every part of the event because Graham could not sit by himself. I was so sad for him, torn inside.

Wanting him to have fun and wondering if watching everyone else hurt him, like it hurt me. It was the last party he was invited to. Each and every one was a heartache for me.

Chapter Twelve

Beyond equipment

Bath time. So many parents love this time with babies and small children. It can be so sweet and intimate. It brings out the soft side of all grown-ups. It was that way with my first two boys. Not the case for our third child. The blood-curdling scream was heart wrenching. Strapping him into a chair that he didn't want to be in was so hard. I felt as if I was doing something cruel.

We could not hold him from the side of the tub, as his tone was so unpredictable it wasn't safe. He could flip into the water at any time. He could slip out of our hands at a moment's notice. So we took turns in our bathing suits in the tub with him. We tried to make it fun by bringing in his big brothers, but the tears kept coming, and it didn't seem fair to put the older boys through the crying.

It was so hard to endure that there was no way it could be a daily routine. We bathed him if he needed it—like if he threw up or wet through his diaper or had a blow-out. Sometimes it was multiple times a day, and others every few days. We learned to be fast and get it over with as soon as possible. Yet another example of something ordinary other families enjoy that was hell for us.

Next would be the other kinds of chairs. Would it be worse than the bath chair nightmare? The chairs: we tried to look at them from a different perspective. A positive one. They represented Graham's independence.

I reflected that all things get easier with time. When a therapist suggested we get a wheelchair for Graham when he was four, I was upset. He was so small he fit in a stroller. I doubted they even made wheelchairs that small. I knew he was not getting one and told the therapist I was not interested.

When Greg and I first went to the Abilities Expo years later and saw all the kids in wheelchairs, I broke down and cried. I didn't want to think of Graham in a chair. Graham was six, and I still couldn't imagine that day.

The Abilities Expo was in New Jersey that year, and it featured over a hundred vendors showcasing all the latest technology and equipment. We found an innovative chair that would raise and lower Graham easily. It seemed like a wonderful option, as he was too small for a wheelchair.

This chair was not used for transportation. It was another chair used inside. I could raise him to my height for the transfer to the changing table, which gave my back a break. I could adjust the height to whatever table we ate at to feed him so he was at our level. We would lower it so he was the same height as his peers in chairs. He could even participate in a kickball game at school, if the school would only let him.

Graham had another chair, exactly the same model, to use at school, purchased by the school district. It's shocking that anyone would refuse to allow a child to participate in such a well-loved childhood game as kickball. But it happened.

School refused to let their chair go outside. We offered to pay for any damages to the chair. We offered to sign a disclaimer for damages. Nothing. We told of multiple stories where we took our chair outside with no problems. Nothing.

My husband drove to school every day at recess and transferred my son to the exact same chair from home, took him outside and played kickball with him. Nothing changed. We implored them—telling them my son had never played kickball in his life before now, and he loved it!

The administration refused to allow it. What it finally took was a lawyer. We had to threaten a civil lawsuit.

Graham had a wonderful experience with his Dad. He learned that his Dad would do anything needed to help him be happy. He saw and felt how much his father loved him. He got to spend a week of recess with his Dad. Nobody else's dad played kickball at recess five days in row!

Why did this have to be so difficult? Why couldn't they do the best thing for my child? Why would anyone deny a child participation in kickball? Why was every single thing a battle? Life is hard enough just managing his care. Where were the people in this world that could help us? Not at that school, that was clear.

Later that year, a part on his transportation chair broke. It was a large stroller with wheelchair tie downs so he could ride the bus with his peers. It was a typical school day as far as we knew. No phone call from school telling us there was a concern.

We own the chair. The same year they would not allow him to go outside to play kickball he was put on the bus in a broken piece of equipment. No one called to say there was a problem.

The tears were instant and fierce when I saw him as he was lowered from the bus, and I realized the strap was broken and he had not been sitting on his bottom safely but rather bumping along on his spine. I could only guess it hurt him because he had no way to tell me.

I could not understand how any human being could care so little about the safety of a child as to put him in danger like this. Where was the bus aide? My horror and hurt ran deep. I could never forgive or forget this. I needed to get Graham out of that school and out of danger. He just wasn't safe there.

Imagine sending your baby to school and worrying about his safety? Most likely you cannot. After all, there are rules that must be followed right? I called the bus garage and was told, "It's not our position to know the equipment of each child and whether it is safe for transport." What? He wasn't sitting in his seat! Clearly they could see that and know it wasn't safe?

"I don't know what to tell you. You will have to check with the school." Great. That's where the problem started. I called the state next to see if there was anything I could do to complain or go on record about this. I was told that because we own the equipment it is not the school's responsibility to make sure it is working—it is ours.

Are you kidding me? If it breaks on school grounds, shouldn't they have to call and report it to his parents? "Well, you would think so." It was as if no one could believe it actually happened. I was exhausted, tired of fighting and scared for my little boy's safety. It was not a good place to be.

We needed a lawyer now. I have always maintained this is not about the adults but what was best for Graham. I wish the school district felt the same way.

After some very difficult and upsetting meetings, we got him into another elementary school in the district because what he needed was not at the school he attended. He needed new therapists and a new look.

Why was he at that school in the first place if it didn't have what he needed? We made a decision that what was most important to Graham at the time was to go to school with his older brother Tysen.

Tysen would say good morning to Graham every day when he got off the special bus that brought him to school and tell him to have a happy day. He would find Graham at school events and that brotherly love was more important than anything else. When Tysen moved on to the middle school, it was time for Graham to move on as well.

We got Graham a motorized wheelchair/stander when he was six years old. We got it from a vendor at the Abilities Expo. We were going to try it at home to see if he could use it.

I watched him wheel over the grass, He played chase with his brothers. He was learning to use a joystick to control it. The joystick was on the arm of the stander. For the time being, someone had to help. His face was happy, and he cried in frustration whenever he stopped. I watched as he learned to take control of his independence. It was bittersweet.

The bitter? Watching my child confined to a machine, dependent on it to move. The sweet? His ability to move independently.

I was checking to see if there were marks on his knees from the equipment when he suddenly pushed forward and knocked me over. On purpose. With a smile on his face. I had forgotten he knew how to move the stander at will and that he was a playful seven-year-old. I laughed and told him he got me!

He could only use the joystick for a short distance. He had tried and tried, but Graham did not have enough hand control to use the joystick functionally.

He could do it a little bit, and we kept hoping he would get better at it...but it just didn't work for him, and we had to accept he could not use this power chair. He was still little and would forget about it. Even if he didn't, he would have no way to tell us he missed it.

The machine sat in our basement and collected dust for a year. That year turned into four years. A reminder of what he could not do. We could not move it because we did not accept that he could not use it. Finally we accepted the broken dream and donated it to a child that could use it.

After the scary breakdown of equipment it was time to move to a new chair. Previously we had used adapted strollers because Graham was too small for a wheelchair.

Years later I remembered seeing 20-30 people at the Abilities Expo riding their wheelchairs everywhere to demo their equipment. I remembered I cried most of the ride home. I could not face my child being sentenced to life in a wheelchair. It felt like the worst news we could get, and it would mean he would never walk. I couldn't face it that day. Eventually the day arrived.

There was a new technology that allowed kids to push to a stand from their chair and then sit again using a spring mechanism that moved with his muscle tone. Pretty cool. He could "stand" or "sit"—his choice. This somehow made the purchase easier for us. It seemed different than a wheelchair. It represented independence for him.

Within weeks, we had problems. It seems they had not worked out all the kinks. It would soon be a nightmare for us as Graham broke the footplate every few months, by the end twice a month.

The lap belt broke every few months, and we had to disassemble the "sit to stand" option—which was the reason we bought it in the first place—as it seemed to encourage a bad tonal pattern and he would get stuck in "stand." So, after a year and a half of aggravation, we put our egos aside and started the process to order a new chair. A wheelchair.

Chapter Thirteen

Beyond dolphins

My child entered the world in so much pain. I did not know how to help him. I felt his pain so deeply and wanted to give him inner peace. I would have traveled to the ends of the earth to find a way to help him. Little did I know it would come to me.

"I may not understand what he is doing or how it works... but if it does nothing more than bring that smile to your son's face, you have to follow this." —Louise Brown Smith, Physical Therapist.

It was the very first time I saw my son smile. With tears in our eyes, Louise and I were gently hitting each other on the shoulder and with unspoken words. *Are you seeing this too?*

I knew I would do whatever it took to bring that smile to his face again, that wonderful, beautiful, innocent smile that had not come for four long years. Not once. That is 48 months or 1460 days without a glimmer of happiness. It was the beginning of our healing process. At that moment in my living room I had no idea what the next eight years would bring. How could I?

CranioSacral Therapy (CST) was a turning point in our lives. When Graham was four years old, we found a local therapist who introduced us to CST. He came to our home to work with Graham.

In the early days Graham would cry endlessly through sessions. My therapist would check in: "How's mom doing?" Somehow I felt the need to be strong for my son and let him work it through. Often I just wanted to cry. Soon he began to spend less time crying and more time squirming and fussing. It took me a long time to realize that crying was his only method of expression. I learned that crying is communication.

In the session we began to talk to him about what he was feeling, and he would get quiet. At this point I wanted to feel what he felt. From the very start I saw the magic of CST. My little boy had been so unhappy, crying non-stop. Graham was not sleeping and unable to be at peace.

The very first time a CST therapist laid hands on him...Graham smiled. Then he laughed. (My turn to cry.) At that moment, I knew it would be a part of our lives forever—if for no other reason than to bring him joy. I was committed.

My therapist in New York told me that the Upledger Institute International likes to treat moms with their kids, so I began weekly treatment as well. CST allowed me to feel all the emotions I kept bottled up (grief, fear, sadness, anger) in order to be strong for my son.

I had a significant SER or Somato-Emotional Release (a memory that comes back) and began to go back to my childhood. I recalled a concussion in high school; I re-experienced labor. CST freed my emotional imbalance enough to show me what it could do for my son.

We were committed, he and I. He received so much therapy that at one point I think we had ten therapists in our lives, and I needed to reduce it somehow. I began to back off CST and found excuses not to go because it was all too much to handle. As I did, he began to have trouble sleeping again, got agitated and just didn't seem comfortable in his body. It was the sign I needed. We went back to CST.

At this point, I had an experience with a dolphin. Things happen for a reason. While in Las Vegas, a trainer asked me if my son and I would like to touch a dolphin. Just show me how! My heart skipped a beat. We approached a beached dolphin, and it closed its eyes and got very still.

First, I touched it; then I helped Graham's hand touch it twice. Then I asked him if he wanted to try to touch the dolphin on his own. I had no idea if he could voluntarily move his own hand to do this. I held my breath and watched. He did reach out with one little finger (it reminded me of the scene in the movie ET). When he touched the dolphin she opened her eyes, picked up her head and put it on his lap.

Chills went through me, and I gasped for air. I looked at my husband to verify if I had seen it. The look on his face said it all. The trainer later told us in ten years he had never seen anything like that...the dolphin they worked with was playful and talked to the crowd, but she pretended to be asleep for Graham.

It was truly amazing. I actually doubted if it had really happened and needed to see it replayed on video to believe it. Greg had videotaped it. The video proved it had happened. It was magical. I knew I had to get to the dolphins.

I told everyone this story about the magical dolphin. I was drawn to dolphins and their intuitive nature. Someone I told the story to remembered that the Upledger Institute International did work with the dolphins years ago and suggested I call them.

We were referred to the Upledger Institute International clinic in Florida for a week long therapy program. Intensive therapy, could he do it? My son was four years old, and intensive therapy from nine to five a day, five days in a row, was not something he could do.

I asked about dolphin work and was told it just so happened they reinstituted that program that summer in the Bahamas. It was only four days, thirty minutes with the dolphins and intensive work in the afternoon, based on the client. This was it. I knew he could do this. John Upledger himself would be there for one session in August. That was the one I wanted to attend.

I called for ten weeks and played a never ending game of phone tag. I finally asked my husband to call every day until he got through, and he gave himself a reminder to call at work. Ten to fifteen messages later, he got a real person on the phone. "We just opened up two more spots in that class today" was what he heard. Graham got in, and we were headed to the Bahamas in three weeks.

I had never read anything Dr. John wrote. I went on faith in what I'd seen happen in our first CST sessions in Syracuse, New York. To have the guy who founded it work with my son? How cool. He would be getting the best of the best.

It would be dolphin therapy through the Upledger Institute International. Dr. John Upledger himself would be there. We were going. How did we get here?

Persistence, perseverance, and faith.

August 2004: Freeport Bahamas with the dolphin in the ocean! Graham was so small I could not let total strangers take my baby in the ocean with giant dolphins, so I got to go in with him.

Two therapists who I'd never met were assigned to my son. We stood on a platform in the water, and the dolphins could approach and touch Graham at will. The first day was a little unsettling. I didn't know what to do, what my purpose was, or how to comfort Graham yet stay out of the therapists' way.

I had never seen multi-hands work before (more than one therapist per client)—I had never seen a dolphin in the water before, let alone a dolphin that put its nose (rostrum) on my baby's head.

Rationally I knew it wasn't going to bite, but I admit there was a sense of fear and adjustment there. Very soon I felt their calming energy. Their intent to help was immediately felt, even by me, a protective mom not quite sure what was happening. We all got grounded.

By day two I couldn't wait to get in the water. I will never forget looking into this dolphin's eyes as close as a person and feeling its energy. Just when I relaxed, Graham tensed. It was a lot of crying, moving, and even spitting up. It was hard to know if the thirty minutes were helping, but the calm nature of the therapists, the confidence in the work, and the amazing process in the afternoon had us ready for day three.

Nobody could have prepared me for what happened next. Graham was in the water with two therapists and the dolphins. I was holding his hand, and he was crying so loud I began to question what I was doing.

Is this even helping him? What am I doing?

No sooner had the thought crossed my mind when a dolphin appeared out of nowhere and raised its body out of the water to put its rostrum on my jaw and send warm heat throughout my body.

I was in shock. I had broken my jaw in college, but nobody there knew that. I was there for my son. I had internally questioned my presence here, and that dolphin answered me in a magical and profound way. That dolphin let me know that they knew way more than humans did, and that they could help—and were helping—my son. I was in the right place. I had permission to heal myself and my son. That moment changed my life.

At another point, Graham and I re-lived his birth. Only this time I got to hold him, love him, bond with him (after the therapeutic birth), while at his real birth he was rushed to NICU. In the afternoon session, which was on land, Graham slid in his therapist's arms, off the table, down my legs and turned over. It was as if I'd watched him being born.

The therapist handed Graham to me—something a C-section does not allow. It was like the doctor handed me my child for the first time. I had no words, just emotion. I cried tears of joy and just held him close to my chest. This time I could cuddle him to me, something I'd never been able to do before.

The respectful manner of those two therapists in that moment was such a gift. No words, just space. They shared an intimate personal experience that I wanted to keep to myself for a while. They smiled, gave us a hug and let us be.

That night, I fell asleep holding Graham with the feeling of holding a newborn, a peaceful content that's hard to describe. Another gift—I had never been able to hold him and fall asleep before CST!

What did we get into? It was overwhelming. Dr. Upledger spoke to his therapists about talking to cells. This stretched my limits, but there was something I felt that told me I was where I was supposed to be. Who knew years later I too would be a therapist talking to cells—it was as if that day he was teaching me too, in ways I did not yet understand.

During that first trip, my son cried and cried, louder and louder. I didn't know what my role was, but I stayed with him, listened to every word spoken by various therapists, took mental notes on what was said and done and journaled it at night. Major changes occurred.

I remember the first time Dr. John walked into the tiny hotel room in Florida. It was August of 2004, and the therapists and clients were waiting for his arrival. The room grew quiet; you could feel the energy change to one of respect as this white haired man entered the room. In the days that followed, I would soak up every word he uttered, listening and learning lessons I would never forget.

He offered to stay with Graham and work on land while the others went to the ocean to work on a boat. That session was the beginning of a special bond he shared with Graham. He suggested that I bring Graham to his clinic in Florida in three months to follow up.

I remember in that setting, marveling at the size of his hands. He asked us to meet him in the Bahamas again, and we were thrilled to see what might happen next. I never imagined that I would become his client too.

In the beginning I was Graham's mom, no name and none needed. He told me he had never met anyone like me. Most people came to him asking him to fix their child, but I never did.

All I was looking for was inner peace. I did not want to change Graham. I wanted to help Graham be happy and pain free. Each time we visited the dolphins or Dr. John there were lots of changes.

I remember another poignant moment when we were at a dolphin-assisted therapy program when Graham was about five years old. Another mom was choked up with emotion, having a hard time talking, and he reached out and touched her. "You are comforting me, aren't you Graham?"

She broke down in tears, as did many of us in the room, witnessing this moment of compassion from a boy who could barely move his hands to touch something he wanted in a purposeful way, as he gently, purposefully, reached out and touched this woman with such love she melted and allowed herself the tears she had been fighting to hold back.

No one moved. You could have heard a pin drop as a moment of such magnitude was felt by those present. Graham silently touched the lives of everyone in that room.

In 2011, one of the therapists noted that Graham read the emotion about five to ten seconds ahead of all the adults and therapists in the room, and he reached out to comfort the person before the rest of us even caught on. Once again, it was truly amazing to see my child impact another life without words.

We were part of a documentary that year. I was asked to present our story with the dolphins and CranioSacral Therapy at the Upledger Institute International's "Beyond the Dura" International conference in April of the next year. It was 2012, and the room erupted in a standing ovation after my presentation. It was moving and emotional, and you could feel the room pulse with hope. My DVD presentation was titled "A Celebration of Healing."

One colleague, Kate Mackinnon, was so inspired by our story that she included us in her book From My Hands and Heart, published in 2013. Her book released on May 1st which is Graham's birthday. After this reaction I knew I was meant to continue to tell our stories.

Here is an excerpt from that presentation in 2012:

"Though my son's cries were loud, I somehow knew that it was okay. Soon the dolphin joined us and Graham's cries changed. Over those next few days I learned to hear the difference in his cries, to see him change and grow and wonder about the wisdom of the dolphin. The cries continued, and the more I heard, the more I worried. What was he feeling?

Graham communicates with his body. Dr. John followed his body and the patterns it presented—allowing the movement, listening to it and learning from it. He didn't try to change it. This was a place where it was safe to feel pain and anguish. No one tried to stop the crying. Instead they were silent witnesses to his suffering.

I began to learn that this was all part of grieving. Allowing Graham to feel it, cry it, and share it—with the dolphins and with us. It was all a part of his process. I began to accept that this was Graham's way of telling his story, that the cries and his movements were his voice.

As a nonverbal child he had no other way to tell us how he felt—how his body felt. Most people try to stop someone from crying, believing they are being comforting. That is not what my son needed. He needed to tell his story.

I heard pain, anguish and sorrow. It was difficult, and it shook me to the core. When it was over—it just stopped. Wow. There were no other words. His was a tale of challenge one so young should not have experienced. I somehow knew he was in the right place. I could feel it in my heart. Surrounded by love and accepted for who he is, he told us his story on his terms."

These words were inscribed in a book called *Lessons Out of School* given to me by Dr. John Upledger (He wrote about Graham and I on page 256):

To Barbara, I admire and support you as a mother—I love and respect you as a human—and I am here for you in every way.
Dr. John Upledger
Founder, The Upledger Institute

When Graham was first born he was in agony, crying all the time. I was desperate to help him, searching for anything that would give him peace. I found CranioSacral Therapy. I found The Upledger Institute and its founder, Dr. John Upledger.

We took him to the dolphins seven times and the Upledger Institute in West Palm ten times. CranioSacral Therapy changed all of our lives. We saw so many positive changes through CST and dolphin-assisted therapy (DAT). Years of amazing stories to tell!

Chapter Fourteen

Beyond craniosacral therapy

When Graham was eleven years old, I sat on a plane headed to a funeral of a dear friend, CST colleague, and a dynamic spirit...I found myself in a place of reflection. Our connections in this life are what I cherish most. In some ways I had known little about Liliana, known to me as Lili.

She had worked directly with Graham only a few times. Yet she and I were somehow close from the first time I met her. Kindred spirits, always smiling and looking for the good in people or the situation. I loved watching her work as she showered her clients with unconditional love.

Through my journey from Mom to therapist, Lili was always in my corner, cheering me on with hugs of encouragement and knowing smiles. (She too was a lay person who became a CranioSacral Therapist, driven by personal experience). It was my privilege to work with Lili both in the Intensive Program at the Upledger Institute International (UI) and the Dolphin Assisted Therapy Program (DATP) in Freeport Bahamas. Her soul is now eternally playing with the dolphins.

I didn't see Lili for a while except at the dolphin programs, and usually she worked with other clients. We actually connected first through her husband Bill, who had a special connection with Graham. Lili shared that Bill had never actually wanted babies.

When they first met he was on track to become a priest. He married Lili, giving up the life he thought he would lead and started a new one. Lili and Bill had two daughters. He just wasn't comfortable with the little ones. He offered to hold Graham to give me a break.

It was so nice to see Graham comfortable with a stranger. It was the beginning of Graham's ability to connect with other people. Eventually, through the years, Bill became so attached to Graham that he began to desire a grandchild of his own.

In a teary heartfelt story he shared this with our group. Some guys are not comfortable with newborns, but Graham changed all that for him. Lili laughed and hit my arm, whispering that their daughters might want to have boyfriends or husbands first! Her eyes were filled with tears, and I felt privileged to witness her love for him and amazed that my son had this effect on this couple.

It was later that I got to work with Lili in the Intensive Program. Lili shared her own story. She had serious heart issues, and Dr. John had saved her life. She then took the classes to become a therapist and give back. We had this in common.

I wanted to share the gift that helped my son with others. I was a bit nervous at first and considered myself "just a mom" with no formal training or license. Dr. John asked me to work in the intensive clinic, and I remember writing on my form I was worried about my lack of knowledge in anatomy.

I was assigned to Lili. Lili smiled and said she didn't know that much about anatomy either and assured me I would be just fine. She told me to just go with what I felt. She was working with a client from Spain. They spoke fluent Spanish for three or four hours.

No words were needed for me to feel what was going on in his body and blend with her to connect with what the client needed. It was intense work and proof that no words are needed to make a profound connection with another human being. I had already learned this from Graham.

Words were not needed to feel the emotion or to do the work, and while I knew this through Graham, it somehow felt deeper and more reverent to connect to this other being without language. Perhaps I chalked up my nonverbal connection to Graham as "mother's intuition." I did not speak this client's language, knew little about his life, and yet felt bonded with him in a way that was deeper than most relationships I have in my life.

I couldn't believe Lili was gone. I posted a You-tube video of Graham walking on Facebook. Lili's husband, Bill, had kept a blog going since his wife became terminally ill and, he posted this:

Grace and Graham

"How do you define grace?

For me it is the feeling of receiving something special, the feeling of being blessed and gifted, especially beyond what I would ordinarily expect or scarcely even hope for.

I have experienced grace throughout my whole life. From the moment of birth on, I have been fortunate enough to have been showered with love, acceptance and respect. Year after year people have come into my life who have enriched it immeasurably with their gifts of learning, caring and even challenge.

It is no surprise that I consider Lili the supreme gift of grace in my life. Her complete acceptance of me and love for me are an experience that was at once so miraculous and so natural that it defies description. Losing her both during her illness and at her death has been the hardest experience of my life.

But even this devastating reality does not mean that grace has disappeared from my life. I still experience blessings every day especially from my daughters and the other members of my family who love, cherish and support me in ways too numerous to count.

But beyond that I see evidence of all sorts of other blessings, graces that soothe the spirit.

Here's one example.

Today the mother of a young boy with cerebral palsy sent me a video. Four years ago, both in Florida and in the Bahamas, Lili and I had worked with the then seven year old Graham; he was a sweet child who loved to laugh but at seven he could not talk, nor really even hold himself upright.

The video, which was taken a few days ago, shows the now eleven year old Graham. In it thanks to the assistance of a rolling chair-like apparatus, and many loving therapists and teachers, Graham is able to "walk"—to propel himself around a room, to play a game of tag with one of his teachers. To someone unfamiliar with the condition of people who have CP, what is shown in the video might seem very limited but, believe me, it is monumental. For someone like Graham who depended on others to literally carry him everywhere, to have as much independent mobility as he exhibits in the video is amazing.

What is grace?

Graham walking is grace.

Lili working for hours with Graham in patience and love was grace.

Graham's mother Barb coming from New York State to pay her respects to Lili at her memorial mass—that was grace.

Having the opportunity to meet Graham and his mother and to have held Graham in my arms for so many hours – and to realize how touched I had been by the example of this young person who could look and laugh and play but without the power of speech—that was grace.

I give thanks for all these things, and I know how much Lili would have rejoiced—perhaps, is rejoicing at the exhilarating new freedom that Graham has in life."

I cried as I read the blog entry. Bill has such a gift with words. He is able to help the reader feel what he feels. Both

Bill and Lili were important to Graham and me. I saw Bill hold Graham with the love a grandfather has for his grandson.

I was touched by that moment. Years later I still see a vivid picture of this in my mind. At an intensive therapy program, when it ends everyone—client and therapist alike—comes together in a closing circle to say goodbye and share thoughts from the week.

At closing circle Bill shared that he couldn't wait for his girls to have children. He did not want kids when he was married. Bill shared the story at Lili's funeral that he told her he could not marry her, and she said, "We would have had beautiful children together" before leaving. Those words haunted him so much that he found her and married her.

Goodbye, my friend. Lili Cunningham was a special person, and I feel blessed to have known her, loved her, worked with her and laughed with her.

Part of why I went to the funeral was to let Bill know how much he had touched my life and Graham's. To let him know he was like a grandfather to Graham, and to thank him for giving Graham the feeling that he was unconditionally loved. It was the only time I saw Bill cry.

So there is an amazing thing that happens when you bond with someone energetically. A blending of spirit evolves into a connection that can last a lifetime...or beyond.

Chapter Fifteen

Beyond guilt

I don't think I will ever be beyond guilt. Being a mom brought out the guilt in me. I would do anything for my kids' happiness, and I put them first without thinking twice.

Some parents feel guilty when they are not watching their child and the child falls off a piece of furniture they climbed up on before the parent could reach and catch them. I did with my first two, like somehow I would be able to prevent every boo-boo and protect my children from the world.

With Graham it was a lot more traumatic and horrifying. He was eight years old when it happened. My child with cerebral palsy, who I thought couldn't move himself off a chair by himself, did just that.

I had left him on a chair to get a tissue (my nose was running), and in seconds he had flipped himself off the chair, hit his head on a glass coffee table and ended up head first stuffed in a decorative garbage can. Yup, you read that right. My child was in a garbage can. How can that happen?

I heard it. THUD. Mom alert on high, I heard a sound that was scary. I ran into the room, but I couldn't find him. Where the hell could he be? He can't move! I looked on the floor, nothing. Then I heard a muffled cry and terror set in. He couldn't breathe. He was in danger, and I *had* to find him.

I was scanning the room wildly, and then I saw his feet, his body stuffed into the basket as if he were standing on his head. I screamed, cried, and pulled him out, and I held him to my body, praying he was okay—not understanding what had happened. He was okay, but I was not.

I developed a fear of leaving him. I couldn't leave him. Even when there was a sitter, I would stay nearby to make sure he was okay. It took a long time, but I eventually worked up to actually leaving the house to buy groceries. My mind was on Graham the whole time I was gone, and I felt guilty for leaving, worrying if he was okay.

It had only taken seconds for him to fall a short time ago. How could I let him out of my sight again? I needed to get over the guilt and separate. That was not going to be easy.

One of Graham's therapists made me feel guilty for not being at her sessions. She made a snippy comment that it would be nice if I attended her sessions. How dare she? There was a sitter there. How is that any different than seeing a child at day care?

She judged me for leaving him. I judged myself for leaving. He was on my mind even when I was physically at a different location. It took years of therapy to be able to leave him with someone else and not think about him, let alone actually being happy or having fun when I was not with him.

I still feel guilt when I am happy without him. I don't think many could understand what it is like to be with him. Almost no other human being on the planet understands that I am rarely ever without him. He is always on my mind and part of my thoughts. Since his birth, he became a part of me. Actually he replaced me and comes first always...

It's hard to describe the feeling. It's like he has taken over: concern about his care and the responsibility of caring for him is ever present. It's an overwhelmed feeling, like you are always behind. There is always more to do.

It's a hopeless feeling, like you can never do enough to help and there is no way to catch up. It's a survival feeling, a fight or flight response, adrenaline running constantly, on guard at all times because you never know what crisis will happen next.

To have another human being completely dependent on you to survive changes you. It was a major undertaking to pass his care on to others. Caregivers, nannies, teachers. Even when I would leave the house, I could not get him out of my mind. I worried constantly. I personally disappeared.

It wasn't until Dr. John Upledger told me that I needed to separate from him or my stuff would start to be his stuff that I was frightened into the separation. The fear of adding to his load was terrifying to me. I didn't want my baggage to be his...this was one concrete thing I could do for him that would help.

John Upledger knew just what to say to me to give me permission to heal...and then in so doing, help my son. I had always put everyone and everything before myself. I lived and breathed to find peace for Graham. I never stopped researching, trying new equipment or therapies—whatever I could to bring him joy. It consumed me.

From the beginning, I had a special connection to him. I somehow knew what he needed. Was it mother's intuition? It wasn't like that with my first two children. It was somehow different. I had a knowing that I had to learn to accept.

Graham introduced me to that side of myself. It had always been there, but I ignored it. I would know that I would win the bingo game before the game ended, or that my name would be drawn for a door prize: crazy things that were easy to pass off. I might say to Greg, "Tell your Mom I need to talk to her." What?

Then the phone would ring, and it was my mother-in-law calling for him, and my husband would just look at me. "How did you know it was her calling?" How did I, indeed. That is the knowing piece.

"The real story is you, Barb; not Graham."

I didn't believe that. Not yet.

If you had told me when Graham was born that it happened for a reason, I would have cringed. How could there be a reason for his suffering? Or mine? "God brought him to you for a reason." *Really? Tell him I'll pass,* I'd think to myself. "Things like this happen to the strong." *Thanks, but I don't want to be strong,* I'd say inside my head.

Today I know in my heart that there were many reasons that my youngest son came to us in this way and that Graham's life changed my life.

Having a child with severe needs that required 24 hour care changed my life. There had to be someone home at all times. My husband worked so it became mostly my job. We did not have help or nursing care. It felt as if we were trapped in our house. I had to find a way to get away without leaving the property. Two things brought me moments of peace and joy. Gardening and family photographs.

I could walk outside and around the house to my gardens. If I only had five minutes to try and get my act together, rebalance, scream or yell....I could go outside. I began to work at creating a space that held continual bloom and changed with the seasons so there was always something new to appreciate. My gardens were part of my healing process.

I also found it soothing to scrapbook photographs of our family. I could create artistic layouts to show our travels, achievements and family fun like sledding or swimming. These books highlighted the happy memories. This was a huge part of my healing process as I felt this was a gift to my family. Every year when I finished, I would sit with my boys and look at every page. It reminded them and me that we had wonderful happy times despite our challenges. I hope you enjoy some of my favorite photos!

Siblings
by the sunflowers

Graham in the
Bahamas

Colby and Graham
sledding

Tyson and Graham on
the Disney Cruise

Barb and Graham

Greg and Graham in
Hershey Park

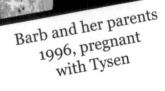

Barb and her parents
1996, pregnant
with Tysen

Barb and Graham at a
family wedding

The dolphin
touches
Barb's jaw
2004

Barb celebrates her 40th
with the dolphins 2004
Discovery Cove

Barb and Graham
with "Papa John" (Dr
John Upledger)
2006

Barb and Graham in
the
Bahamas 2004

Barb with her boys
on Cape Cod

Graham in
pre-school

Our special
connection

Graham in his walker

A mother's love

Our family

Barb
and Greg

Barb and Graham,
Grand Canyon

Greg and Graham
chillin' out

Graham with Elmo in
Sesame Place

CHAT Club at
Syracuse (SU)
University 2013

Graham the
teenager

Chapter Sixteen

Beyond the device

How could we understand him? We just did.

We tried everything out there to communicate with Graham. There were switches (you hit a button and it voice activates) to teach cause and effect. He was not interested. There were computers you touched to voice activate, he could not use them. It was a painful few years trying to reach him. He laughed appropriately at jokes, he followed our conversations.

I knew he was in there, but how would I get the rest of the world to see that? One day we heard about something that worked with your eyes. A local agency (AccessCNY, formerly known as Enable) hosted an informational session showing parents and professionals how eye gaze technology worked.

As the sales rep began explaining how the computer worked, my eyes glazed over. He was way too technical for me. It all seemed cool, but if the person could not calibrate the program, it would not work. Game over. To calibrate, the person's eyes have to follow a bouncing dot across the screen. If Graham could do that then he could use eye gaze technology.

I called the sales rep from my car as soon as his presentation was over. I asked if he could test Graham at our house to see if eye gaze was an option. He was able to get there to try and calibrate the machine with Graham.

We held our breath and watched... We saw the bouncing dot appear and Graham's eyes watch the screen. When it was done, the report popped up to show us the results.

And he did it.

He really did it.

Then the salesperson programmed a picture of a chocolate lab, asked the name of our dog (Diva) and programmed the computer to say "Come here, Diva." All Graham had to do was look at the picture of the dog.

He did it...and so did Diva.

She came over, tail wagging, covered him with kisses, and I cried. He did it. He had a huge grin on his face; he squealed with delight and happily watched Diva wag her tail. Even Diva knew this was a big deal. He could use this. We had finally found a way to communicate with him! We were thrilled!

We learned that Graham could calibrate the eye gaze computer so next was figuring out if he could use it. We did some research and discovered a facility in Florida that had a dolphin experience and a classroom experience and they worked with eye gaze computers! It seemed like fate had sent us to the Keys to find out if this would work.

In April 2009, we took our vacation in Florida and brought Graham to Island Dolphin Care. Island Dolphin Care is a not–for–profit organization that is dedicated to helping adults, children and families who are dealing with developmental and physical disabilities, emotional challenges and critical, chronic or terminal illness.

Graham and his brothers Colby and Tysen got to swim with the dolphins. Graham learned how to use his eyes to make choices for fun. For the first time in his life he could choose between a number of options and there was no wrong answer. (This would be important to remember later when school tried to use the device only to test him. He was either right or wrong. He could not use his device to socialize.)

There were notes from his therapy sessions that said things like this: *Hello Graham and welcome to your first classroom session at Island Dolphin Care! On his first day*

Graham came into the classroom with his whole family, Mom, Dad and his two brothers. His brothers sat on both sides of him.

Graham used eye gaze to choose to paint his families hand prints. He got to choose who to paint and what color to paint their hands. (This picture of our families hand prints hangs in his room today).

After this fun adventure we knew he could use eye gaze to communicate and started the process of buying one for him!

Things felt like they were out of our control. Our relationship with Graham's school was horrible, so we couldn't ask them to buy it for us. At this point the administrator said no to whatever we wanted so asking the district to support this was not an option. Not to mention it was incredibly expensive.

We wanted to do this right away without asking anyone's permission. We wanted to do this the right way, without fighting with them. We wanted to reach our son no matter what the price. We were lucky enough to be able to purchase it on our own, and we did.

We thought everyone would be as thrilled as we were that he could do this. We were stunned at their response. They would only use it for yes and no. This is a computer that does way more than that, but we had to swallow hard, thank them and agree to start there, at yes and no.

They did not want to learn a new program called VS Communicator, which is how he learned to use the device. Instead they asked us to reprogram the entire device through Boardmaker, which was already familiar. We wanted them to use it so we paid someone to reprogram the entire device.

After using it this way for a while they decided they liked VS Communicator better and asked us to change it back. Of course we did. So much time and money was lost. They did not understand how to use the device and it cost Graham.

This school told the administration that we were changing the programming. As a result, the district wasted tax payer dollars buying the exact same computer so they could control programming.

All they needed was to create a separate user name but they were not trained properly and would not listen to us. One of the most difficult things for parents to navigate is their emotion. We were angry and upset but telling them that would not help us or Graham.

Privately we considered this therapist head strong, inflexible and not trained well enough for this device; but if I said that to her, we would be considered difficult parents. It is so hard to restrict your feelings and watch what you say to protect people's feelings who just don't care about yours.

We want the best for our child. It's perplexing and bewildering to me when my child doesn't have every opportunity to be his best or excel in all situations. That's what happened here. My heart is heavy with the frustration of why the school couldn't just help us with Graham's device.

Typical students have years where they have a teacher they like or one they don't like. You tough it out hoping that next year will be better. With therapists it is so much harder. There are only a few so if you don't gel with the therapist you might have him or her for four years and what do you do then?

Some therapists are good and some are not so good. Sometimes it's a style, or different training or lack of training that is challenging. Sometimes well- meaning adults make mistakes.

We had no idea at the time we were in for years of fighting with this school. We didn't realize that many of the folks there just did not believe in him. They did not know how to use the device properly and kept telling us he could not do it. Then it shifted to "he might be using it at home with you, but he doesn't want to use it at school."

We didn't understand. Why would he not use it at school? We tried to figure out what was different. He could use 6-8 buttons at a time, but they restricted him to two, like yes and no. He could not show his abilities or communicate to his present level of performance at school and I had to find a way to change that for him.

I was desperate to get them training. Unfortunately, the company only had sales people, and the training they gave was mostly how to program the device, not how to work with a student.

We paid our nanny to work on the device. She didn't have training either, but she believed in Graham and was tech savvy. One day over the weekend I discovered a game on the Tobii (his eye gaze computer) that was called catchmii.

It was a Saturday and I was fooling around with the device checking out new pages and programs that I had not used before when I saw the icon for catchmii.

When I opened it up I realized it was a game to check someone's abilities to see different parts of the screen. It had positive reinforcement with sounds and cute animation. You could advance to different levels. It started with two buttons on the screen. If you looked at both you advanced to four buttons, then eight and it kept going.

Graham did amazing things! He got through several screens, proving he could see more than I thought he could. I was thrilled!

School was not. I asked them to try it with him, but sadly they would not let him advance from the screen with the fewest buttons to the harder screens with more buttons. Somehow they decided he needed to achieve looking at the two buttons at a certain speed.

They would not advance him to the next screen with four buttons until he did it fast enough on the screen with two buttons. That made no sense. We didn't care how fast he was using the device. We didn't ask for him to use it at a certain speed. What had happened?

We were trying to show them how many buttons he could see on the screen but we failed because they would not allow him to show what he could really do. What would we do next?

Why do adults tend to limit Graham's ability to communicate? This was another case from my viewpoint, of yet again, his ability to communicate being limited. Didn't they get it? They just didn't. I had to find someone that did get it.

We had found a therapist in 2011 that could help him, but the school refused to work with her. None of this made any sense to us. This therapist worked with several school districts in the area and had always had a positive experience helping students use their devices at school.

She told us that most of her students had their peers' pictures and names on their devices so they could socialize with them at school. Our district refused, and until legal action resulted, Graham did not have the opportunity to communicate with his peers. All of elementary school he was denied this, and to this day it breaks my heart. We were at an impasse.

We hired a lawyer to come to our meetings. It did not help the way we hoped it would. The school continued to refuse to use the device with more than two buttons, restricting his communication.

The school refused to work with our home Speech and Language Pathologist (SLP), who is an expert in this field, simply because we recommended her. This had been happening for years but now it was about his communication and we could no longer play games with the administrator.

We had no choice. We had to take legal action to get Graham what he needed. We did not want to take this path and had tried every other option available to us to no avail. I interviewed six law firms. I chose someone who had never worked in the area, but was the dad of a special needs child.

Greg and I decided we would prefer to lose with someone who understands this life and tried his best then to choose a high priced jaded lawyer who was negative. We will get to that story later.

Chapter Seventeen

Beyond my limitations

When Graham was ten years old, I was thrilled beyond belief that he had a way to communicate with the world through his eye gaze computer. It was a huge computer on a rolling stand. It was difficult to move around and I had no idea how to program it.

I struggle with technology, and I was unable to help him in this area. My mind went blank when I tried to read the directions. I didn't want to admit how hard it was for me, and perhaps I was stuck because I didn't want to talk to my child through a computer either.

I asked Greg to take the lead on helping him to understand how to use the device, but he didn't. I could not understand why he didn't, and it felt to me as if it was not as important to him. I pushed, pleaded, begged and annoyed him until he would sit down and help Graham a bit... and then he would seem to lose interest.

It took a toll on our relationship. We yelled at each other. We had no patience and fought a lot. We disagreed about everything. Now I realize maybe he was having the same emotional block I had.

School was not able to help him and I refused to give up despite my limitations. We bought him the smaller device that would allow him greater access to communication because it would be mounted to his wheelchair. He no longer depended on someone else to remember to bring it, turn it on etc. It would be a part of his wheelchair now.

I was so excited for the day Graham's smaller eye gaze computer would be mounted to his wheelchair and he could finally say hello whenever he wanted to, not just when someone mounted his device for him. He had a mount that was on wheels almost like a rack that clothing hangs on that his device was mounted to with his first device.

It needed to be wheeled around with him but was so big you needed two people to transport Graham and his device, so it could not travel with him at all times. It sat in certain classrooms and was only used some of the time.

This smaller device could mount right to his wheelchair, and he could use it any time he wanted to. I wanted to go to school and watch, but something inside made me stay home. I knew it would be disappointing.

When I read the note from school I found out most of the day was spent trying to figure out how to mount the device and position it. He barely used it. I am so glad I didn't go. It hurt and I felt alone. Greg didn't seem too interested in how it went. I felt this ache of sadness that this was not something we were experiencing together.

Ever since Graham was born I had tried not to set myself up for disappointment by readjusting my expectations for the people working with Graham and not hoping for as much. As I waited for the school to figure out how to mount the device, I called tech support to try to set up training that I was informed would not happen for at least a month and a half. Why? There was no rep in our area.

He was using it, but it seemed what he could do was limited to what the adults allowed him to do. He gave a weather report at school to his class using the device. I realized that he could help spread awareness of his way to communicate by public presentations.

As co-chair of the Special Education Council I was supposed to give a report to the Board of Education about our committee and the year's events. Graham was ten years old and in first grade. I was sure that none of the board members had ever seen someone talk with an eye gaze computer. I asked if I could bring Graham.

To promote disability awareness, I brought Graham, and he addressed the Board of Education in his school district, presenting his story and introducing his mom all using his new eye gaze computer. It was an emotional night that I will never forget.

When I asked Graham if he wanted to present, he smiled and was excited when we practiced what he would say. I knew what words he would say because we practiced it together. I was not prepared for his emotions the night he did his presentation. After he introduced me, he squealed with delight. I was choked up by this. You could feel his excitement and pride.

I remember how touched I was by the teacher of the gifted program, who through her tears told me how thrilled she was to hear Graham's story. She has worked with my older two boys through the gifted program and could see that he was gifted too, just in a different way.

Graham has a support system that most people will never have. As I posted his success at that public presentation via email and Facebook, comments from friends around the world began flowing in.

The night he presented to the Board of Education, the room was filled with support for my son. New friends and old, neighbors, teachers, therapists new and old—it was an incredible outpouring of love, support, and one of my moments...the kind you never forget.

I knew I needed to find help. I needed to find someone who could use this device with him and prove to the world he could do it. Not just use it, he showed us he could do that. I needed someone who could help him advance his communications skills. He was limited by the school staff.

He was only allowed to use two buttons at school when at home he was using many more. They did not believe me so I knew I had to find a professional to help him. It would take me a while, but I would find her. Someone close to me said they had heard about a speech therapist who might be able to help him but wasn't sure. I called anyway.

Around November 2011, I found her. Her name was Beth. I knew right away she could help Graham. However, she worked for several school districts and didn't have a lot of time.

We took whatever she could give us and started the process. I don't think Beth had a lot of hope for Graham at that first appointment. I gratefully took whatever time she had available to work with Graham.

She thought I was exaggerating what was happening with Graham at school. She had never had any difficulties working with anyone in any district before. She was shocked at how she was treated.

Graham was so frustrated with people not getting him that he had shut down. She hung in there though, and one day Graham showed her he could use the device. His trust in her built, and he began to show her his sense of humor.

Chapter Eighteen

Beyond letting go: could we do it?

At one point during those dark days when we were struggling to understand how to help Graham communicate on his eye gaze computer, I thought to myself, *So if I can't do it, Dad can't do it, and his school can't do it... what then?*

I put the thought out there that I wished I could just take him somewhere and immerse him in communication with people who understood how it all worked. I got online and started researching camps or schools. *Sending Graham overnight?* I never would have dreamed that I would ever consider it. But it was exactly what he needed. It was time.

He was ten. He was in no danger anymore. He was on medication to control seizures, and the people running these schools worked with and cared for kids like Graham all the time. Graham required full time care and assistance with all personal care issues. Could he do it? Could we do it?

I discovered a school in Pennsylvania. I picked up the phone and spoke to the admissions counselor. Even thinking of sending Graham to camp was a huge step...but calling? I surprised myself. I thought, *if this is what he needs then it doesn't matter how I feel, how Greg feels, or how his brothers feel... We need to put his needs first.* So in May we went to visit the school.

To see 56 kids all in wheelchairs with ages ranging from 6-21 all in one building was overwhelming. Almost all of them used power chairs. We saw one girl operate her chair with one tiny finger. Wow.

Graham tried one long ago but couldn't use the joystick so well, and we put it in the basement to collect dust with the label "dreams that can't come true." But if she could do it with her pinky, maybe he could use a power chair? Wow. Renewed hope and we just walked through the door.

The thought of Graham working with teachers and therapists that had the experience of working with so many children like him was exciting. Most of them had been there for ten, twenty or even thirty years! We toured the dorms and saw the exact bed we have at home with a wall mounted TV, also just like at home. I knew he could do this. Now to fill out the forms, figure out the logistics and tell the school.

I explained this as a rite of passage to Graham. "I can't believe you are old enough to go to overnight camp! I feel so old!" He giggled. To others, I said it was an opportunity for him to see people like himself and to improve his communication skills. Our hope was that this experience would teach him to communicate with his eye gaze computer.

So how could I go from being worried about sending him to an all day camp in North Syracuse to an overnight camp in the state of Pennsylvania? Easy. It was best for him. Taking your own feelings out of it, ignoring your comfort level and helping your child to the next step of independence is not easy for most parents. It is ten times harder with a fully dependent child.

Still, I knew he was socially ready for this. So it became a matter of fact course of action. It was just the next step in our journey. Thinking of it as the next step gave me time to bury my apprehension...until the day I actually left him.

Now thinking back, age ten was about when we sent Colby to overnight camp. This was different, I knew, but it was time to move him to the next step in his path and admit we could not help him take it. He needed to go to the "experts."

Our hopes were that bringing Graham to this school would make the difference for him in becoming a communicator. We were hoping his competitive nature would kick in when he saw all the other kids using devices to talk. We held our breath and crossed our fingers.

Letting go of Graham, allowing him to experience a sleep away school independently was one of the hardest things I have ever done. There are times when you have to let your typical kids have more independence. I cried when Colby, my first child, got on the bus for kindergarten, not sure how he would find his way from the bus to the front door without me.

Later when he was 15, I put him on a plane to Aspen Colorado to participate in the Teen Socrates Seminar at the Aspen Institute, and then sooner than we knew we would be looking at colleges.

I think the difference is that you are more a part of the transition to independence with a typical child. You pick their outfits until one day they do. Then you explain why plaid and checks don't go together, until you hear why they don't care if they match.

Soon they care what store they buy their clothes at, and they are wearing cologne or perfume...then dating and overnight co-ed parties. That's not exactly how it was when I grew up, but we learned to roll with it!

It was harder with Graham as he is nonverbal. The cues were not always there. He wouldn't say, "Mom, Barney is for little kids..." or "I don't like that anymore" like his big brother, Tysen. The clues were there though, if you looked closely.

You would see his head turn at Snow White at Disney World and realize he had a crush...she kissed him on his forehead, left bright red lipstick marks, and he was delighted! Suddenly there was a note from school telling us Graham liked a "hottie." (What does that mean at 11?)

How would strangers know what he needed if he could not use his voice to tell them? Was he hungry? Thirsty? Tired? Happy? Sad? This next step was huge. Nineteen days without him. I couldn't have believed I would ever be able to do that, and somehow I did. I did it for him.

I remember when I sat Colby and Tysen down at a local bakery to explain about the overnight school and sending Graham away. Colby said, "I don't know if I can go without seeing that kid for 19 days!"

I asked if he could do it if it was the best thing for his little brother. While he was thinking about that, Tysen said "I do not want to make a decision about where Graham should live when you and Dad are gone."

I said hopefully we would be around for a long time, and that day was a long ways off...and then explained that if it did happen while Graham was 21 or younger, he had this new wonderful place to go to so their lives would not be affected by caring for their younger brother.

Wow. Conversations that are difficult for adults, yet my kids are facing things I never did when I was their age.

Off we go. So we got the check list, packed and labeled his clothes and equipment, and loaded up the car. Off we went to PA! Everyone seemed surprised by how calm I was as we set up Graham's room, unpacked his things and filled out endless forms, answering tons of questions.

I would be fine until the moment I was not, and everyone would know it. I was determined to hold it together and not let Graham see me cry.

We were showing the nurses how he lays in bed (the position, the pillows around his body, the angle of the hospital bed). Tysen leaned over kissed his brother and said, "I know you are going to have lots of fun, buddy." Then it was time to say goodbye.

I had not heard Graham laugh since we arrived, and more importantly, no one there had heard it either. So I tickled him until he laughed, and I said, "Now there's the Graham I know." I could then feel the emotion about to erupt like a volcano and turned and left the room in a hurry.

The social worker with me cried when she saw my tears, telling me it reminded her of leaving her own child at college!

I knew it would be hard. I had no idea how hard.

I had held it together through setting up his room, meeting the team that would care for him, answering the ever so difficult and annoying question: "What does he like to do?" I hate that one. How do I know? He seems happy to do anything, try anything, as long as he has company. Pretty difficult to determine what he likes and dislikes when he cannot talk and has limited access to everything.

When I gave them a tense response, the social worker looked at me sympathetically and asked me if I was okay. I told her I was fine, but my thoughts were racing.

Am I over sensitive today? You bet. I am leaving my baby, who I have worried over for 11 years, 24 hours a day, with total strangers. Yes, it's a state of the art facility. Yes, every kid here is happy. All 56 kids are in wheelchairs. Does any of this help? No. He is my baby.

While I had tried to look cheerful the whole day, the reality was that I had to train a whole team of therapists, teachers, and nurses to do what I did every day. Hello? Was anyone getting that? I did all 25 of their jobs by myself just to give him what he needs to survive, let alone "playing."

My head knew this was the right thing. A great experience for him. My heart broke wide open. Ripped apart when we saw him look over his shoulder as we left.

Later that day I sat quietly on the deck at a beautiful hotel in Hershey Park. I needed to be alone. Greg and Tysen needed to ride roller coasters and scramble their brains. Boys. I was surrounded by them.

Guilt set in fast. Feeling like I abandoned him, having left him in an institution where no one knows him. It didn't matter that I went to overnight camp for eight weeks when I was only seven, four years younger than Graham was now. I loved it. This was different. This was Graham.

So the next few days were tough. We received a call from the school and learned they were not feeding him enough. It was taking too long for hardly any calories. At home he would drink 26-52 ounces of liquid daily, plus 8-16 ounces of water and some pureed food.

The camp counselor said they were getting in 4-6 ounces of calories tops, plus water and tiny bites of puree." With that many kids there, how was my kid the only one they couldn't feed?

They conference called Greg and told him we needed to come feed him over July Fourth weekend. He was so upset he could barely tell me what they said.

I did not want Graham to think he failed and they called his parents to come get him. I called Jenna, who was in her residency in PA. Jenna worked with Graham while she was in medical school. Jenna was like family. She could drive there after work and get there by 8 o'clock.

We skyped a feed with the therapist before Jenna arrived. First off, Graham looked like he thought he did something wrong and they called his parents to tell on him. I had to reassure him it was okay. We couldn't breathe until we saw him laugh.

That didn't happen until Dad put his head down on his hands in frustration, showing his bald spot which the therapist pointed out, and Graham giggled. Whew. Okay, we knew he was okay.

On to the show. I had never skyped. It was so strange to see faces in the computer. Graham was so serious. The therapist stood behind him with his head against her belly, arm around his head to support it. There was no one in front of him and suddenly a hand appeared with a cup full of liquid.

I wish we had talked about how they supported him before I saw it on the computer. It looked like a football choke hold to me. I was horrified. I was on camera, so I forced a smile and said, "So I am noticing that you feed him differently than how we feed him, and I am wondering if you would try it our way." I talked her into the front, feeding him on the right side like we do at home.

"I don't see much of a difference," she said.

I had to stifle the x-rated comment that popped into my head, and instead said, "Great, so you can try it this way for a while" without skipping a beat. Breathe.

The next surprise? Lip closure. We let Graham do his thing and we did not care how dirty he got and how much food and liquid spilled out of his mouth. He spills a ton. Sometimes he covers us with liquid as he swallows and spits. It just became a part of our life. It was who he was and how he ate.

We accepted it and didn't really notice it any more. So now imagine someone closing your jaw every time you swallow by moving your chin up to close your mouth. It was very invasive of his personal space and very different—and hard to watch. I didn't want to criticize her or tell her not to work on lip closure.

This method worked for her with her other students, so I joked about what a neat eater he will be when he gets home. I said to Graham, "I know this is different. Different is not bad or good, it's just different." We said goodbye and ended the video skype call. I ran to the phone and called the nurse.

I explained how different this was for him. No one touches him at home when he swallows, and now he has someone moving his jaw every swallow. These were two huge changes in how he is fed, and it was no wonder to me he was having trouble.

He ate well with us during the skype call, and I felt better. I got a text from Jenna who had been stuck in traffic. I told her to turn around, go home and head over on the weekend. The emergency was over; we had just seen him eat okay.

Jenna told us they were asking why he didn't have a g-tube when she visited that weekend. Well, when he was little he could eat by mouth, and we did not want to go down that path. He had grown at his own rate and always increased. Maybe we needed to revisit this.

So on Friday night at 9:30pm the registered dietician called. She was a matter-of-fact person who laid it out for me. "We need his rate of height and weight to increase at the same pace," she said. I was to send her the past growth charts on Monday.

No one had ever looked at it this way. I knew immediately he was growing in height but not in weight. With typical kids as long as they are growing you don't worry. Not so in this case.

The dietician reassured us that she expects kids to lose weight their first week of a residential experience. Wow. I wish I heard this a week ago. I might not have cried for two days in a complete panic that my child was starving.

She also told me it is common for kids to hit this bump in the road at adolescence and that several kids about his age just got g-tubes. *Thank you for making it feel better,* I thought.

We picked Graham up and had an appointment scheduled with a feeding specialist in New Jersey on Monday, and an appointment with a new GI doctor on Tuesday. The summer had set us off on a new course. We hadn't planned on it, but we were grateful to have the insight that he was struggling and he didn't have to.

Then the guilt came again. I looked at him, two years younger than Tysen when physically he looked ten years younger. Should we have done something sooner? Again, my head knew I had been working on finding a way for him to communicate for the past ten years, yet my heart broke thinking he could have been growing.

You can't get that time back. I learned long ago that we could only handle one thing at a time, and we picked communication. It was time to pick growth.

Chapter Nineteen

Beyond g-tubes

The g-tube dilemma: Back in 2002 and 2003, I had learned about g-tubes (gastrostomy tubes) while taking Graham for his Hyperbaric Oxygen Treatments. There had been a child with a g-tube there.

His mom poured liquid into his belly where a tube had been inserted. I was horrified. It was infected and oozing pus at the site of a plastic button that had been placed in the child's belly. I remember I was grateful at the time that this was one thing we didn't have to face.

Several months later, a local GI doctor suggested we give Graham a tube to increase body weight. We refused. "He is gaining," we had argued. "Maybe not the way you would like, but he has not plateaued in weight." Until there was a flat line in growth or a failure to thrive, we refused to go there.

I thought about how many parents didn't know they had a choice to do that surgery and just did it at their doctor's suggestion. Frightening.

I tried pureed food again, and he was doing pretty well until we had a setback. We got hit by a pickup truck going 95 miles an hour. All three kids were in the car.

We spun out of control, doing two complete 360's as the airbags deployed, glass shattered, and wind whipped through the car. It was April 10th 2007, and I was on my way to my in-laws' house to celebrate Grandma Tresness's birthday. I never saw the truck coming.

I was driving an SUV and was three quarters of the way through the intersection when he sped over the hill and into our car, with a baby in a car seat in the front of his vehicle. Miraculously, the baby and he were fine.

The way I knew my kids were alive? I mentally heard each child crying and I thought, *That's Colby, that's Tysen, that's Graham—we're good.* Then I drove the car into a stop sign to stop it from spinning.

My dad had taken me to a parking lot when I was 16 and practiced spinning in the snow so I would remember how it felt. I was so grateful for that lesson. I was not worried about the car or how it was moving and could focus on my children. I jumped out of the car to physically check the boys. All three were crying hysterically, but it seemed there were no physical injuries.

Graham's door wouldn't open. As my vision really took in the scene, I realized that his side of the car was damaged and that was why the door would not open. *Not Graham, why Graham?* I panicked, ran back to the front to climb over and get him out of his car seat. I needed to hold him, look him over and know for sure he was not hurt. By this time two ambulances, two fire trucks, four police cars and a helicopter were on the scene.

Rescuers were freaking out looking at Graham's low tone. I tried to explain he had CP, but they weren't listening. I got into the ambulance with him to try and calm him down. They had his head strapped to a board, and his tone was kicking in, making him cry and arch. I was frightened he would choke.

I had to scream at them to pull over and allow me to comfort him or it would all be over because he might choke to death on the way to the hospital. They finally listened.

We made it to the hospital and met Tysen there. I had to choose between my children because they had to go in separate ambulances. It hurt like hell, but I had to go with Graham. We all went home that night, shook up but physically okay.

The very next week Graham threw up all day long, every half hour, and was admitted to the hospital for the Rota-virus. He could not eat. Slowly we got him back to formula. He wouldn't drink water. He kept refusing.

I learned this is not unusual for kids with CP. They do not drink water. No one seemed concerned about his lack of water intake, except me. I knew it was important but had no idea how to help him. Finally, during one of our many trips to the Bahamas for dolphin therapy, an osteopath I met from Spain advised me to give him a sip every time anyone else had a sip of water. Eventually he would take two sips, then more.

She was right. It worked. She also shared it would reduce his drooling. The medical community had suggested I put him on more drugs to stop the drooling.

I opted for water, on the advice of the beautiful therapist from Spain, and I am grateful that she met Graham. It worked. The kid who would only take a sip of water ended up drinking eight ounces a day in elementary school. He did not drool. Yes!

I learned long ago that I can only handle one major change in our routine at a time. Graham began his new communication device, so we put feeding on hold again. His caloric intake was fine—he was growing and while still very small, that had to be enough for now. One major thing at a time was our rule, so solid food was on the back burner again.

Ten months later, when we went away for February break 2010, he ate pureed gazpacho. He ate shrimp soufflé. He ate crème bruleè.

If it was a pudding consistency or puree, I gave it to him to try. I got school to try pudding and applesauce. He never looked back. We gave him solid or pureed food for seven months straight! At his new summer program, they pureed whatever was on the cafeteria menu and tried it with him.

His therapist set it up for the fall at his school that he would finally go to the cafeteria and eat with his peers at lunch! Or so I thought. I would later learn that her idea of being in the cafeteria was all the special needs kids and their aids sitting at a table together, segregated from their peers.

You see that is just it. "Peers" to her meant all kids with special needs sit together away from the "typical" kids. So much for the concept of inclusion. At least he was allowed in the cafeteria.

The next year he was fed in the back of the school in the therapy room because the therapist needed to train staff how to feed him in private.

"Why? Are you embarrassed to feed my child in public? It might surprise you to hear that I feed Graham at the mall, at the movies, in restaurants and in public at all times." I demanded that he be allowed back in the cafeteria, but the first few weeks of school had come and gone and I couldn't get that time back. The damage had been done. Graham was labeled "different." No kid wants that label.

It was 2011, and he was still not very big. We hoped we could add weight and were open to trying anything. Our GI doctor told us kids with g-tubes have a pre-digested liquid that adds calories. I'll never forget the look on his face when my husband said, "Okay let's try it. Go get two glasses." Greg tasted it himself; the doctor couldn't do it. He laughed and said, "Tastes like chicken... No, actually it tastes like shit!" Graham tried it for a while, but it didn't really work.

We tried smoothies, Ensure, whatever he would drink. We saw nutritionists that suggested various ways to add calories, including olive oil. We started pureed food again. He was drinking 3-4 cans of Ensure daily to keep calories, minerals and vitamins up.

It was a lot of work; it looked weird when he would eat, but we kept trying. We were not seeing as much weight gain as we would have liked, but he hadn't stopped growing so we kept doing what we were doing.

With time, my feelings on a lot of things changed. The g-tube is one of them. In 2011, after that summer away, we knew the time had come. We had to face the g-tube. Before we did, we went to NJ to consult with a doctor.

That doctor explained that until we got control of his elimination, a g-tube would not help. Feeding and elimination go hand in hand. If you are constipated, there is no room for food. How could Graham tell us if he was constipated? He cried.

We focused on that and got him going daily for the first time in 11 years! Our hope was that if he was moving his bowels regularly, he would be able to eat more.

We held our breath and hoped that regular bowel movements would make more room for food. No such luck. So off to another new GI doctor for more tests. We discovered he has slow gastric emptying. It takes him extra time to process what he eats. That explained some things and added yet another medicine to his daily routine.

The hope was after a few weeks on that medicine he would be able to eat more. Several months passed, and he did not gain any weight. Heavy sigh.

Graham's elimination has never been pretty. We would get calls from his school regularly. To quote Tysen, "Some people are so stupid." I got a call one afternoon because Graham had a blow out so runny it hit the floor. Gross. Pause.

"Do you have a change of clothes for him?" I asked. This was me trying to figure out why they were calling me. She said they did. "I'm just worried it might be contagious to the other kids," the school nurse replied with a heavy sigh.

I forced myself to breathe. To resist the urge to burst out laughing. "Nope—constipation is not contagious. Neither is diarrhea. We give him medicine to regulate his bowels, and I guess I gave him too much this morning."

I then had a moment of sympathy for the person who thought he was sick. "He is not sick. He is battling chronic constipation. We are seeing a new doctor and are trying new meds to clear him. We obviously gave him too much," I reassured her.

"Well, I'm just worried it's contagious to the other kids...you know, the feces on the floor." My moment of sympathy was over. Really? I had to resist the urge to say, "Then clean it up."

Instead I explained that now that he has cleared he is done, so let's just leave it as you will call me if he has another problem. I stopped short of saying anything else, although I really wanted to share my frustration and anger.

We had accepted how Graham ate and just saw it as a part of who he was rather than accepting that it was a difficult thing for him.

We had heard this from a staff member at the overnight school but still could not see how hard it was for him. We needed the wake-up call. It was hard for him to eat and it took a lot of time and energy. We could help make it easier for him.

Parents and families that had g-tubes were very supportive. For us, it was not the road we wanted. There is just something foreign about putting a plastic tube in your kid's stomach to feed him that we didn't want to deal with. It was another thing that made him different.

Sure, we knew we had to, that it was the right next step and would help him grow. It still sucked. Intellectually, I knew it was the right decision. I hated having to make it in the first place.

I don't want to feed my kid through a tube. There it is. I said it. I was okay with other kids that had tubes, but that was not for Graham. He was able to eat and that was that.

Okay, he could not eat like the rest of us, but he could still use his mouth and eat. We pureed everything, and lots of times he spit it out...but he still ate. I was desperately holding on to any shred of ability to do things, not at all seeing how hard it was for him to do it.

If you had asked me if I would do anything to make life easier for Graham I would say yes. If you asked me to put a tube in his stomach to feed him I would say no. He can do it. Was this about him or me?

When we could finally hear it was hard for Graham to eat and that he put so much energy that he could put into other things if we made eating easier for him, we got it. Wow. It still was not our decision to make; it was his.

We asked him what he wanted to do. Most parents don't ask their children what they want. They make big decisions like surgery without their kid's input. Not us. It was Graham's choice.

We asked him if feeding was hard for him, and he answered yes. Graham told us he wanted to try the g-tube, and that was all we needed to hear. Surgery it is. In 2014 the g-tube was a good decision and made administering meds and feedings so much easier. It made our life caring for Graham easier.

Chapter Twenty

Beyond accessibility

I have learned important life lessons from Graham about nonverbal communication, disability rights, and lack of awareness regarding accessibility, to name a few. Here is a little bit about how I took those lessons as a gift, and found myself on a journey of healing that enabled me to help others on the same path.

It can happen anywhere: at a sporting event—a track meet. The path to the stadium seemed like it went on for miles. Stare after stare; I walked along pushing the wheelchair and feeling alone. When I finally arrived at the stands, the metal ramp seemed to draw even more attention to us as we rattled and rolled to the handicapped section of the stands.

Heads turned and eyes darted away, not wanting to be caught staring, until we reached the accessible seating. Somehow there the isolation was a bit more comforting. Above the track, away from the mainstream traffic, we were no longer a spectacle.

One brave soul visited every track meet. Graham's teaching assistant came over to say a warm hello with a smile that let him know she was truly happy to see him. I was so grateful for the company and the warmth she brought to us. She will always have a special place in my heart.

There was one time it was more difficult than usual. It was an unexpected event as we thought it was an away meet.

Sometimes, when your guard is down, it hurts more. That day was one of those days. One of our older boys didn't acknowledge us. He spoke with his older brother and his dad, but hardly glanced at Graham or me.

I tried to wave twice, but he was off with his friends. I wondered why we came to see him. He ran his race and again, no sight of him. I texted him when we arrived and also when we left. It made no sense to stay because the wheelchair couldn't get to his other event. So we walked/wheeled out alone.

Why did I put us through this? Again, I felt responsible and guilty for the pain, as if I could have known we would be hurt somehow and stopped it. I wish it were that easy. Was he truly ignoring us, or did he just get caught up in the meet and having fun with his friends?

I think he was just having fun—and because we are always on display and ready for the hurt, it was easy to be hurt by this too. Graham's brothers love him. Our lives are harder than other families, and sometimes we forget that they just need to be typical kids for a bit. Here is another example of Graham's effect on the world:

One day at the track and field days at this elementary school, his presence affected the crowd of spectators. I used to dread these events because he didn't fit in, and his differences were highlighted. This year was different. I began cheering for each and every child I knew that was special. In years past, I joined the silent crowd, quietly cringing and observing them "try their best."

Not this time. I had changed. I didn't think about who was there. I didn't care. I wanted those kids to hear me cheering and to know that they had support.

An amazing thing happened. When it was Graham's turn to start a race by walking on a gym mat in his adaptive walker, I couldn't cheer. I was holding my breath, hoping he didn't get stage fright and freeze. They introduced him on the microphone.

He had to take ten steps, which for him was like a 200 meter walk. He smiled, but he did not move. Everyone was still. It was quiet, and then I heard someone say "Go Graham" ever so quietly. People started to cheer and clap.

Soon we were all cheering, mom included, and as if he were waiting for his fan club to do their part; he took those steps, smiling all the way, sending a feeling of achievement throughout the crowd. He had waited for the crowd to cheer for him. In that moment, he brought us all together in a way I will not forget.

When Graham was 11 years old, we went to dinner to celebrate my mother–in–law's birthday. She picked the restaurant. There is an accessible ramp on the deck. The last time we went there it was winter and the ramp was not shoveled.

They lifted my son in. I was upset but turned my head the other way. Why was I upset? The law states you need a ramp, and that it is dangerous to lift a person in a chair. We were headed back to the same restaurant, but it was summer so I thought we would be okay.

This time was worse.

It started as I wheeled him around because the ramp is right next to the building, and all the people at the tables along the window stared at us. I tried to make light of the situation and laughed, saying, "Here we go again, Graham. Everyone is staring." Then we got to the door, and it was locked. I just stood there with my mouth open. We had called ahead to tell them we were coming with a guest in a wheelchair.

My in-laws had not made it back around to the bar area, so no one knew we were standing there waiting to get in. There was a table in front of the door. The guest at it stood up and unlocked the door.

Just then my mother–in–law came into the room and yelled, "Oh my god, the door is blocked. Let my grandson into the restaurant this instant!" Still no staff in sight. The way the tables were aligned, five tables of guests had to stand up to allow my son's wheelchair to pass through. That was about half of the dining room, and it was quite a scene.

I was so angry, trying to keep my cool as it was supposed to be a night of celebration. This was a violation of the American Disabilities Act (ADA) and the fire code, and no one seemed to care.

I asked the staff person standing by our table if he was the manager that night, and he said yes. I proceeded to retell the story, ending with "It was an awful experience." All he could say was he was sorry.

At the end of the meal when it was time to leave, I could not handle another scene. Tysen and I went out the front door long before Greg and Graham left. Thinking this was the appropriate way to handle the situation, the manager came over and bellowed through the restaurant, "Person in wheelchair coming through, get out of the way."

He meant well but should not have yelled about the disabled person leaving the restaurant but instead quietly facilitated the exit. This kind of thing is so tiring.

Later in 2014, Greg and I were at dinner at the same restaurant, and guess what? The door was blocked by a table of diners, again. I commented that the accessible door was blocked, and that was a shame. I was told the deck was under construction.

I could see there was no construction near the ramp. It was clear that this was an ADA violation. I did not let it go. I said, "I care because that same door was blocked when I tried to bring my son in his wheelchair here. Even though we called ahead." The staff person told me to call ahead and ask for him, and he would personally make sure it was open for me. A nice gesture but he missed the point.

That is not what ADA compliance is all about. Without words Graham touches lives, brings hope, comforts, expresses love and shows others the way. Why do we go back? It's great food. We will always be advocating for something.

Chapter Twenty-one

Beyond seizures

How do I start to describe a night of terror? I thought Graham died...then that he *might* die... then wondered if he would sustain brain damage.

It is hard to describe how frightening it is to watch someone you love have a seizure. You desperately want them to look at you to know they are okay, but they cannot.

At age 10, Graham had a seizure that was over a minute long and scared me. It happened on a boat in the middle of the Caribbean. When he had the seizure in St. Lucia that February break (2010), we had no Diastat (his emergency medicine) or any way to help him on the boat.

I was scared that I could have lost him. We had no medicine to stop the seizure, and we were 45 minutes from a hospital in a third world country. What struck me at that time: He could have died. We had relaxed into a comfort zone that he was fine and had not brought his meds on vacation. Talk about getting scared straight.

It was the first seizure that Colby witnessed. I saw him watching on the boat. He had a scared look on his face. I knew he had questions, but I could not focus on him. I could barely control my tears. I cried the entire ride up the hill to our house.

When we got home I knew Colby was rocked, and scared. He paced around the room and finally said, "I have a difficult question for you, Mom." I asked him to wait a minute, poured myself a stiff drink and said, "Hit me with it."

"What's Graham's life expectancy?"

The truth is we don't know. We talked into the night about seizures, cerebral palsy, death... It was a long, emotionally draining night.

Greg wanted to return to the island for April break. I put my foot down and stated that Graham and I were not going back to St Lucia in April. His life was worth more to me than the trip. This experience felt like a premonition of sorts. Seven months later on Sunday, September 26th 2010, Graham had a seizure well over five minutes, then another for ten to fifteen minutes.

Greg administered Diastat, which we had never done before. He really had no way of knowing how long Graham had been seizing before he got there. Thinking that the first dose did not get administered as it felt like air coming out of the syringe, he decided to give another one.

At this point he had calmly called for me to come upstairs. My anger at not being called immediately would surface later.

Twenty minutes of hell. Colby, then age 15, was holding Graham when the meds we gave him (Diastat) kicked in, and his body went limp in his arms. Colby thought Graham died in his arms. I watched it, not sure if he had died, my heart breaking for both of them. I quickly felt a pulse and knew he was alive.

I screamed for Tysen, age 12 at the time, to tell Dad to call 911. Our house was filled with strangers, the circle in front of our house a mass of flashing lights and rescue vehicles. The picture of our little boy (35 lbs., 10 years old) comatose going up the driveway in a stretcher is burned into my brain.

There was a blur of lights and a surreal feeling as I made my way to the ambulance, pronouncing that I was going with him. I rode in the front, looking through the glass window at my child, barely breathing, an oxygen mask on his tiny face, wondering if he would survive this.

No one told us what would happen if we ever had to use the emergency meds. It would have helped to know he would go to sleep. Maybe it seemed obvious. Had we known its effect, the stress would not have been so great. On our way to the hospital I heard the men in the back say Greg had administered two shots of Diastat.

"WHAT?" All eyes were on me, as it was apparent I had no idea what happened. Soon each of them became a husband or a boyfriend defending the fellow man (a humorous moment in the midst of anxiety), as I heard things like: "It won't hurt him, he'll just sleep longer."

To me, the realization that Graham had been seizing for well over five minutes, and Greg gave him the meds before he told me was the bomb. When he did call to me, it was in a calm voice: "You should come upstairs..." I remember asking if it could wait as I was on the computer. How could he not call me first?

A few days passed before I could tell him how angry I was about this. I told him to stop trying to handle things on his own. It was my right to be a part of that moment. If Graham had died I would have never forgiven him. We fought and slept separately that night. The stress on our marriage is huge.

This seizure was more severe than anything I had ever seen before. It is frightening to watch someone you love have a seizure. They cannot focus or see through their eyes or control their movements. It is unclear if they hear you, although I always speak as though he can hear me.

An adult friend of mine shared that she had control over her thoughts but not her body when she had seizures. This time I just held him tight to my body hoping he could feel my presence. I let the fear and sadness consume me and cried hard.

I have never been able to let it in like that, always being strong for the kids or keeping it together until the crisis was over. It was so much better to let it all happen, feel it and let the raw emotion go. I was hysterical and yet focused.

I faced the fear of his death head on and let him know how I felt and accepted my feelings. I remember standing in the driveway looking into the blur of lights from the ambulance thinking it wasn't fair.

Graham just got to point when everything was going well for him. He was finally communicating with the world through a computer, and he had everything in front of him now: it just couldn't be happening, not now. I realized his life would always be like this. It would never be easy for him. It hurt so bad to feel that deeply in my being.

It will never end for him or for us. There will always be the possibility of something scary or life threatening happening. I had to learn to accept I could not control it. Each time I got through something I hoped we would get through it and put it behind us, but it will never be behind us. The unknown looms in his future.

So now we were in a new place. We have always known he was prone to seizures. He had not had one longer than a minute prior to that night. Intellectually, we know all it means is he now takes seizure medication to control any future activity.

Emotionally, we all faced his death and each of us has to navigate those feelings.

Chapter Twenty-two

Beyond puberty

Wow. How did I get here? Slowly. When you count every calorie for years and accept weight gain growth of one pound per year, your child slowly grows. As long as he grew, we would hang in there with him.

Yes, he was small, and people called him a baby. We could get through all that. We gave him every chance we could to let him develop the natural way. When his weight gain stopped then we did surgery to give Graham a g-tube to help him eat. Then he grew over ten pounds in one year. Yikes.

Some parents choose to stunt their children's growth. One of my clients told me they had decided to do this for their son. I was shocked and horrified. I had to remain neutral and try not to judge their decision. It was not easy. They give them medication to stop them from growing so they can handle them.

I could never do that to Graham. I try not to judge other parents decisions, but I had a tough time with this one because you are messing with nature.

Other parents are so fixated on growth that they choose to get a g-tube for their kids early so they look like other kids. We chose our own path and are happy we did. It was harder, but we know in our hearts that we tried everything in our power to help him eat naturally.

A nutritionist put a new spin on this for us when she pointed out how much energy it took Graham to eat his meals. What could he do with all that extra energy if we made eating easier for him? What could he do indeed?

Making life easier for him was not how we had looked at the surgery. Once we did, it was a no brainer. We are happy with that decision and have no regrets about our timing. Now, new challenges pop up that we hadn't met before.

How can I hold him? After 40 pounds people require a two person transfer. That means two people lift the person together. Who would help me?

We needed to install lifts in our home. I had to accept that I could not hold my baby again. It had been eleven years, and this was not going to be easy...but I could do anything for him. I would get through this too.

I began relying on my oldest son and my husband to pick Graham up or transfer him to be changed. How does this work if I am alone? Yup, you guessed right, I got hurt.

One time I decided I had enough strength to lift him. I threw my back out. My husband still does not use the lift. He will not let go of his little boy until he has to. I get that. I am jealous, I suppose.

Graham has blonde hair, so hair growth on his legs just wasn't that noticeable. His feet started to smell after a day at school. Could it be hormones? Is he going through puberty? Soon he was giggling at pretty girls and watching the teen shows with great interest. I guess so. What we didn't know was right around the corner....

We arrived in Disney for Thanksgiving break in 2012 to celebrate my father-in-law's 70th birthday. The trip had been planned for well over a year. On the first night we settled in to our room around 11pm. Graham woke up suddenly and had a seizure.

We couldn't believe it. Not now, not here in this magical place that had always been a happy place for us. I slept on the floor that night, if you can call it sleeping. With every move he made I was on high alert to see if he was okay.

We were headed to Universal Studios to Harry Potter World the next day. What did we do? Bucked up, pretended all is well and headed to the park. Graham seemed off. I tried to reason that it was the seizure, and he would be okay

He was tired and spacey, not at all the way I had hoped he would see the magical world of Harry Potter. I'm not sure he even enjoyed it, as he barely smiled. My heart was heavy, but we pushed on for the other boys and tried to have some fun.

As we left the park, Greg and I decided to take advantage of our caregiver's presence and sent her to the room with the boys to do bedtime while we went to watch the fireworks at Magic Kingdom and enjoyed some wine at a restaurant we like at the Contemporary Hotel. It was a lovely hour of peace.

We talked about how different our life was from everyone else's, how hard it was to face seizures and pretend that all is well when it is not. Little did we know it was the calm before the storm. It was an hour. One hour. We started our trip back to our hotel, the Polynesian. We stopped at the bar at our own hotel for one more drink.

The cell phone rang. It was Colby. "Mom, Graham is having another seizure—you need to come home." I screamed FUCK. Yes, that word came out of my mouth at a Disney hotel.

I was on high alert mode again. I ran out of the bar, yelling to Greg to pay the bill—he was seizing, and we had to leave. We were above the room, and I flew to the door in what seemed like minutes to them, but not to me. I was pissed he was in trouble and I wasn't there. Guilt set in fast.

I was angry that my 17 year-old called instead of my caregiver. Where the hell was she? Why didn't she give him his meds? She should have called us—not my son. It's easy to be angry and place blame when you are scared, and I was scared. No, I was terrified.

When I came into the room he was seizing. Not like he usually does. This was different, and I was frightened. Full body shakes. They told me he came out of it and was cold. I told them he was still seizing and to help me get him up on the bed (he was on his inflatable bed on the floor).

I briskly stated we needed to administer the Diastat and call 911 and was floored when Greg said no. He wanted to wait. He gave Graham the meds but didn't want to make the call yet.

I was lost for words. I could not understand why there was even a discussion. I would later learn that both Greg and the caregiver did not realize the medicine says to call if you have two seizures within a 24 hour time frame.

If it's just one seizure there is a time frame to wait and that is why they wanted to wait. Somehow I knew this was different and made the call myself. What they thought was shaking I knew was a seizure, a kind we had not seen before in Graham: the grand mal.

The paramedics arrived, and off we went by ambulance to the children's hospital. No one does it like Disney...the ambulance appeared out of nowhere. He left by stretcher and a door closed so no one could see the ambulance. They would only take two family members, and there was no way I would take Colby away from his little brother's side so I ran hysterically to the front of the hotel and hailed a cab.

The cab driver explained to the hotel guests he was supposed to drive that night that this was an emergency and my child was taken by ambulance to the hospital. They could see me crying and looks of sympathy washed over their faces as we drove away. I cried the whole way there.

In 12 years he had never had back-to-back seizures. This was new. It was a seizure I hadn't seen before. What did it mean? Was he in danger? We later learned he had "focal seizures" in the past. The second seizure was a general or "grand mal" full body seizure. It was terrifying to watch.

What had happened? Why this new kind of seizure? Why two in a row? Our answers came shortly as we were told that puberty can spike seizure activity. I thought, *Great. In addition to acne and hormones, our kid gets more seizures.*

He finally got admitted to a room. It was 3am and technically Thanksgiving when I convinced Colby to leave with me as there was only room for one person to sleep over with Graham. Greg stayed.

We spoke by phone about every hour, consulting with the neurologist. She explained the puberty experience and encouraged us to stay on Keppra as long as he could, as it is the drug with the least amount of side effects.

This was empowering as we had just been told locally that Graham was nearing the end range of his current drug and we would need to switch. We now knew we could fight to keep him on it longer. So out of the negative came a positive. Keppra had the least amount of side effects. Keppra it is.

We were in a new place. This seizure was his most involved. We knew we needed to see our local neurologist to prevent more seizures. Breathe.

Chapter Twenty-three

Beyond support

You think your support network is strong. Tons of friends, lots of family...then your child is born with multiple disabilities, and no one knows what to say to you. Lifelong friends don't visit. Family members stay away—or better yet, they say, "He's fine—you just always believe the worst about everything."

Or my favorite parent comment: "I don't know how you do it. I could never have done it." *Did I really just hear that from my own mother? Okay, not my favorite thing to hear. Thanks for nothing.*

I used to give people updates on Graham every time I talked to them, even though they never asked. Once I recognized this, I suddenly realized I had to stop. They didn't want to know. Not really. Wow. I couldn't believe it. Once I stopped offering updates, no one asked. Occasionally I got an obligatory, "How's Graham doing?" But that was it.

The support network I thought I had disintegrated. Friends and family were uncomfortable around us, did not know what to say...so they said nothing. We could not go out and felt trapped in our home taking care of this very needy child.

I had no one to talk to outside of my husband. We didn't have that kind of a relationship. I had never needed it before. The stress in a marriage with typical kids can be a lot. Try a child that cries constantly, doesn't sleep, is fully dependent on someone else to care for him and has three to five doctors and four therapists to manage. We were in for years of stress.

We learned to accept that we each deal with fear, anxiety and stress differently. We might yell, cry, stomp off in anger...whatever it takes to get through the moment. The next day we accept each other's method of coping. Sometimes we talk about it, and sometimes we don't. We are in different places.

To others it might seem like we were fighting as a couple. To us, we were just coping. It was not about us. This was about me. I had to learn to help myself.

I have found tremendous benefit in seeing a therapist since 2004. I used to roll my eyes, thinking you had to be pretty messed up to need to see a therapist to talk about your problems.

After I mentally hit rock bottom, emotionally overwhelmed with my life as it was, I tried it. It felt strange to share personal information with a stranger. Soon I began to trust the process, and I learned how great it felt to share my thoughts and feelings without judgment.

I am grateful to the three therapists in my life that helped me find balance, a way to cope with my life, and eventually become more in touch with my own needs as a person, woman, a human being...and not a mother or a wife.

It has taken a long time to get in touch with her, but now that I found her, I feel stronger and happier than ever before. There is a bittersweet catch 22 with this: other parts and people in my life may or may not have grown with me.

I started talking to a social worker provided by Early Intervention. As my case worker said, "I waited until you hit rock bottom before I suggested it." *Why was that again? Did I need to be desperate for you to help me? You wanted me in enough pain to be sure I needed help? There is something totally messed up about that.*

Talking to a stranger about your feelings is not an easy thing to do. It helped though. Having another perspective from someone who was not emotionally involved helped me to see that there were lots of ways to look at things when I was so overwhelmed.

She became my closest friend, which is a sad statement because it was a one-sided relationship. It wasn't appropriate to have any other kind of relationship, and yet she was the only one I could tell how I really felt.

I didn't have time for other relationships. I was managing so many just to get through my son's day that there was no time for anything else. Friends fell to the wayside. We stayed home most of the time because we were too exhausted to do anything else.

It got easier, but we had to accept everyone where they were. Some people talked to Graham, some talked about him, and some ignored him.

He couldn't give any feedback to let them know he heard them so it grew increasingly difficult for people to attempt to talk to him. There were some who always talked to him, even though he couldn't respond—and I greatly appreciated that, as I know he did.

It is amazing to see him interact with people today. He is a confident communicator. He uses his communication device at school, at home and in public more than ever before. We made it. He made it.

I spent the first ten years trying to find a way for him to communicate, and I wondered what was next. I discovered that the next step was connecting Graham to his community through my work with a local therapist.

In 2014, I am with one therapist who has helped me find my way to the inner knowing or the source. Thank you, Paul, for being a part of my journey. This was an email I sent to thank Paul, to honor his role in my transformation and new found awareness.

Life is about connection with others. It seems like a simple statement, but when you truly feel its meaning, it is powerful. I have spent years working to understand this concept.

Many of us learn this lesson from loss, or as we age and are reflective on our lives. Today, for me, it gave me the inspiration and hope to help Graham connect with his world.

I am filled with new ideas on how to connect him with his family, his school and his community. While I have always noted the impact Graham has when he connects with someone, I have felt and seen the visible change in someone who watched his connection with mom, dad or his brothers; I had not looked at how to open the connections for him.

I was driven to help the world see him as I did, know him as a cognitive being, and then crushed when that didn't change much. It was not until this morning that I realized what I was grieving was the lack of connection. Everything changed today.

I feel so much lighter as this new sense of purpose became clear. Ironically this sense of connection is what I love about the work I do, what drove me to achieve the dream of practicing CranioSacral Therapy (CST), what I could not feel myself with many who are closest to me.

More than any person, I know Graham has the knowledge that he is truly loved by so many people. I feel my balance has returned. I know how to go forward without the sense of urgency, but rather importance.

I realized today that this concept has always been my purpose and wish: to help my son connect with the world. I've raised my children to connect with all people as people and not to label others by their race, disability or disease. That ultimately what I hold dear in life are those connections.

Chapter Twenty-four

Beyond Graham: A gift for me

The young man who came to my house to do CST was a physical therapist. I was at the point where I would have tried anything. I barely remember what he said or how he described what he did. What I will always remember is how Graham reacted. He was two or three years old, and it was the very first time I had ever seen him smile. I was speechless.

What had just happened? I sat next to the owner of the company who was the one who recommended this person to me. She and I both had tears in our eyes as she reached out to tap my shoulder and said something like this: "I may not understand what he is doing or how it works...but if it does nothing more than bring that smile to your son's face, you have to follow this." I listened.

Within twenty four hours two people recommended CranioSacral Therapy (CST) to me for my son. I took it as a sign. I had never heard of it before. That was 2004.

Graham screamed non-stop in the car. When I heard that a therapist could come to our home, I was hopeful. I listened. I did follow it (CST). I followed it all the way to the Bahamas.

The first time he was with the dolphins was August 2004, and it was magical. Shortly after that we saw him do things he had not been able to do before. One night at dinner in a restaurant he reached out and grabbed a butter dish and smashed it to the floor. The wait staff came running to help pick it up. We were thrilled he did it at all. He held his head up longer. There was more to come in the following few months.

One day that fall I called a friend over to get some pumpkins. I had been to the $1 a pumpkin place and had a lot of extras that I did not need. They were on my front lawn when she and her teenage son stopped by to pick some up. I came outside with Graham, who was now four years old, and sat down on the grass with him supported on my lap.

The young boy, Alex, wanted to make Graham laugh and started being silly and tossing a football around. Graham started to giggle. We all smiled. He giggled some more, and we giggled too.

All of a sudden Graham pushed to a stand and took two steps. Then four steps. I was supporting him under his arms, but he was doing the walking. I stared in disbelief. My friend Lisa, who is a nurse, asked me if Graham had ever been weight bearing before.

I shook my head and did not say a word. Lisa told her son Alex to do it again. Sure enough, Graham pushed to a stand again and took ten steps. Lisa and Alex were delighted, and then she turned to me and asked me why I was not saying anything. I told her I did not want to jinx it. I was watching my son take his first steps.

When his Dad and brothers came home, I told them what had happened, and we tried to get Graham to do it again. He did it! Everyone was so excited that night.

We told his school the next day, and they tried to get him to do it with no results. He did not do it again—not even at home. It was heartbreaking. We were so excited for him, and then so sad for him. It hurt.

I did not want him to think I was disappointed in him. I decided then and there that I had seen him do it and somehow, someday he would do it again. I did not know when, but I would not give up on him.

Would he ever walk alone? I had no idea. I didn't care. How did this happen? The only thing we did different was

CST and the dolphin therapy. That had to be what unlocked this for Graham.

Dolphin Assisted Therapy has helped Graham do so many things we never thought he could. Graham could not use his arms the way my other boys could. I had given up on feeling his hug. Then one day, my son held on to me in bear hug style as we got out of the water after therapy with the dolphin.

He was eleven when I got this special hug. When I carried him out of the water, he held onto me in a way I had never felt before. Tears free-flowing down my face, time was suspended for me. No one there knew why I was so moved, it was our private moment.

I never wanted to let that moment go as it was a true gift of love. While his arms could not reach out to hug me, that day I felt his hug deeper than any other I had before. No words were needed to feel his love.

Graham has seen therapists from all over the world that practice CST. I wanted to understand it, took courses and became certified as a therapist myself. I am a practicing CranioSacral Therapist and have shared this gift with my community by opening a business.

I reflected that this gift had come full circle. In 2013 a four-year-old child came to me as a client. I request parents stay with their kids and participate in the sessions. After one session, the mom asked if she could make an appointment for herself.

As I worked with her on a significant piece in her healing journey, it struck me that this child led to her mother's healing just as Graham, at age four, had led to my own healing. My heart was full!

The following year, in January of 2014, I attended a therapist retreat in Florida. During that trip the therapists present were all working on issues relating to their mothers. I thought to myself I hope my kids are not working on issues related to me when they are adults!

I did not have any concerns with my own mother at that time. Two weeks after that trip all of that changed (I will get to that later). Back to the animals. The first day we visited a local rescue facility for big cats. Kevin Rose, who was the first therapist to work with Graham and the dolphins in 2004, when Graham was four, practices CST with the animals through his business the CATalyst. It was an incredible experience to be in the presence of tigers, leopards, cougars and bears.

It was life altering for me as I connected with a black Asian leopard named Makoto. Makoto brought me to the realization that his life was always full of fight or flight type situations, as he could be predator or prey at any given moment...but that he could also find that neutral place of balance.

I had been in search of that place within myself, and Makoto showed me how to access it. It is there; it always has been and always will be. My life will always be filled with drama or trauma, but my balance and peaceful place will always be there inside.

Right before I left the area the black bear stood up directly in front of me. All 400 pounds of her. She stood about 6 feet tall. It was as if she invited me to stand in front of her and feel her power. Looking into her eyes was an incredible feeling.

Belly to belly with a black bear: channeling my momma bear energy for sure! There was only a chain link fence between us. This was an experience beyond any other, to be that close to a wild animal, more powerful than me but gentle at the same time.

I was not scared, I was awestruck and grateful for the experience. It sent chills down my spine. I sent pictures to the boys, and Colby said, "I guess you are good with animals." I replied, "That was why I survived raising all boys!"

There is truth to that jest.

For 10 years I had been focused on Graham—mobility, communication, toileting, digestion, feeding, seizures and meds. Inner peace and happiness were all I wanted for him. He was in there. He truly was.

He knew he was loved. He was at school and communicating on his own. He had relationships with his classmates and teachers that I did not even know. He had inner peace, or so it seemed.

From 2004-2014, my journey with CranioSacral Therapy brought me to this point in my life. It is time to close that chapter and move on to the next journey. I am on sabbatical from Ultimate Yu, my therapy business.

I will always help those in need and answer the call of a desperate loved one asking for my help, but my efforts need to go toward the next step now. I set out to give back the gift that was given to me and my family, and I achieved that and more.

Chapter Twenty-five

Beyond grief and dying

In 2011 I took a course on Death and Dying in Manchester, New Hampshire. I followed my feeling that I needed to take the course. Through over a decade of grieving multiple things with Graham, I thought I had pretty much grieved it all. Curious as to why I was still drawn to the course, off I went to NH.

I knew from my profession that people grieve all kinds of losses: job, marriage, disease, death. I had dealt with so much grieving in my own life, as well as my clients. So why was I there?

My father had Alzheimer's disease. They say it is harder for the caregivers and the families of those who have it than it is for the patients, and I would agree. The person is mostly "happily confused" asking the same questions repeatedly.

Not knowing where they are or what is happening; they lose touch with the world. It wasn't until the Thanksgiving of 2009, when my mom and dad stayed with us, that I realized he had declined severely and that my mother was in denial.

He could no longer order his own food or even recognize what was on his plate. She most likely did not realize she was ordering for him and felt she was just reminding him what he liked. They had been together since they were teenagers.

I watched the disease take his dignity, his daily functioning, and his physical body. Yet through it all, he always held the door for my mother to walk through first. He forgot everyone's name but hers. It was a sweet love story.

When Alzheimer's hits, you are in a strange place of grieving the loss of the person who you knew and loved while they are physically present. Their bodies still work but their brains are turning them into someone else. Sometimes mean and nasty behaviors come out, and it is difficult to accept that your loved one is not knowingly doing or saying these things.

Taking care of a parent and a child with serious health issues simultaneously is no easy task. Nothing has been easy for me in very long time.

So how to do you grieve for someone who is still alive? It's much like divorce or job loss. The complication is that the person still needs to be cared for. So, in this course I faced the loss of my dad as well as Dr. John Upledger, who was like a father to me as well.

I knew the last time he worked with Graham and me that he was dying, and we would never see him again. I wish I didn't know. He died several months later, within months of my dad's death. I knew the last time I saw my Dad in September 2012 that we would never see him again and that was the last hug I would ever give him.

I cried hysterically as we drove away from the home my parents both lived in. He had Alzheimer's and lived in a home with my mom that had a memory care unit attached so she could take care of him in the apartment but had supports for other things.

My boys asked if I was okay, and I said no. I explained that I knew my dad would die and that was my final goodbye to him. He died four weeks later.

I delivered his eulogy. I have an older brother and sister, but neither one could do it. I was the youngest by nine years. I chose a picture of him in his younger days and told a story of a man whose personality was larger than life. It was.

He had a good life. He was a typical New England conservative, a chauvinistic man who could barely touch on emotion. He could say I love you. He could enforce his rules:

"my house, my rules." He viewed the world as black and white. There was no gray for him.

I do not remember my parents playing with me. I experienced childhood with my children as if it was the first time. I loved it all, the art, the stories, the imaginary play...I could play with my kids. I did not learn how to play when I was a child, at least not that I can remember.

I attended summer camp for two months starting at age seven. School vacations I spent with my aunt and uncle or my grandmother so my parents could travel on golf vacations.

I remember my Dad making me sit on top of the couch and pick the scaly dandruff out of his scalp with a comb. It was disgusting. I cringe when I think of it now.

No child should ever be made to do such a thing.

He had strong beliefs and was incredibly judgmental, but he was a loving man, and my favorite memory of him at the end was one of him playing with Graham. He was a kind man, and very social. He lived life to the fullest with many friends.

He provided for his family, gave back to his community and it was difficult to see him decline physically and emotionally. However he said loving things to me at the end that he had never been able to say before. It was a strange sensation. He was a different person.

He shared little about his life with me. So it was a surprise for me to learn that he was in the military. He served his time in Upstate NY, which is where I live now. Again, a surprise. He had a military service, and the burial was straight out of a movie, with the young soldiers folding the flag and thanking my mother for her departed husband's service to his country. It was hauntingly beautiful to hear the gunfire salute and taps played at the cemetery.

What would happen to my mother? Her entire life had been devoted to his care. That generation was different than ours, and she truly was out of a job. What now? We suggested she stay at the Alzheimer's home the first year, as there is much to deal with after a death.

At 80 she would need to learn to care for herself now. Her days had always revolved around him. The grieving process took almost a year, and then her own health began to fail.

The last several years have been rough, starting in 2012 when my Dad died in October. 2013 was a rough one too. Graham had a major seizure in November, and it was the night before Thanksgiving. Needless to say, Thanksgiving sucked.

In December Graham had a three day EEG. We found out he was having more seizures than we knew. What we saw as tone (an uncontrolled muscle pattern) was tone nine out of ten times...but that tenth time was a mini seizure that could only be seen on video or by brain wave. Great. "Silent seizures," they call them.

The doctor said he wanted to be proactive to treat this and chose to add another seizure drug called Depakote. Graham reacted to it immediately and threw up the night he was discharged. We called the neurologist on call, and he said to slow down the dosage. We did.

He was still reacting, but not vomiting. At the next increase he vomited so violently that it got in his hair, nose, eyes...I thought he would choke on it. We were all done with Depakote. I called the neurologist and that office told us he had a GI bug and it was "definitely not the meds." So, I called the GI doctor. Thank *God* the nurse we got at the GI office knew better.

She told us to call the neurologist's office back, go over the head of the person who told us to call the GI, and talk with a doctor or someone who would immediately know it was a reaction to the drug.

Graham had several scary life-threatening reactions. Every time I called about a reaction, the response was to treat the symptom with a new drug. They ignored the signs and put his life in danger. Our pediatrician intervened. She called the neurologist personally to get answers.

This was the first doctor to advocate for us in this way. She was frustrated that we were not getting answers. The neurologist then said that Graham needed the second drug to protect him from a seizure of irreparable damage. What the fuck? Our pediatrician yelled at that office for what they put us through and for not saying he was at such a risk in the first place.

Graham had a life threatening reaction to Depakote before they heard our concerns. We got him off the Depakote and on to another drug. Next we faced a nose bleed. I thought Graham would choke on his own blood and die in front of me.

Fortunately Greg has had nose bleeds forever and was strong enough to hold him and stop the bleeding. He was able to pinch his nose and stop it. I could not. I was terrified. I needed a plan for when I was alone. An emergency back-up plan. I knew if I were alone I could not have stopped the bleeding. What if it happened at school?

I remembered Tysen got a bloody nose at practice one day, and they used "packing material" to stop it. I needed to find it. I called the pediatrician, and she told me OB tampons were the packing material.

Okay...tampons it was. They were now everywhere in our house, at school, and in his bag on his chair. If he has a nose bleed, we insert the "packing material" or tampon in his nostril to stop the bleeding. Okay, we had a plan. I could breathe. Crisis over. New stressor coming soon.

On January 26th 2014 I got a call from my brother that my mother was in ICU. He did not have a lot of information to offer. I tried to contact my sister who lived close by but got no answer. I flew to Boston the next day to find out what was going on for myself.

She had a heart attack and was receiving oxygen. I flew there and back in the same day. I had to figure out what came next. I lived in Syracuse, NY and she lived near Boston. How could I help her? How often did I want to visit? Her body was now failing her. Once again I was at a crossroads. What to do?

In February a routine visit for the cat at the vet turned into a biopsy of a growth and the end of life talk for my dog,

Diva. Her liver has been failing for over a year but was now only a matter of time before she would die or we would have to put her down. We went on vacation (our school break) and left a DNR if she got worse while we were away.

We took Graham back to the overnight school for February break so that he could train on driving a power mobility chair. It was our first February break without Graham, and we took Tysen and a friend to St Lucia.

Graham was all smiles when we left, happily greeting people with his device when he arrived. We have all come a long way in a few years.

Everything was going great at school, and when we had skyped with Graham he laughed and let us know he was happy there. I had resolved the issues with my mom and the home. We went for a sail the next day, and as the captain got the boat ready, I got a call on my cell phone. It was the school.

They assured me Graham was okay now but told me they had to administer oxygen. He had a respiratory incident and his oxygen levels dropped below 80. My face drained of all color, and I remember saying "well that's not good."

Everyone on the boat stared at me as it became obvious that something was very wrong. Graham had suffered a respiratory incident at school and had to be given oxygen.

During that vacation I dealt with my pet dying, my mother's heart condition and my son's surprise respiratory situation. I thought after the first few days of stress related to my mom and the dog and their situations that I could finally relax.

So much for feeling safe. More doctors, more equipment, more to learn. Not relaxed.

As it turns out, it was an important thing that happened. We did not know Graham struggled with oxygen. This was a documented incident by a medical facility that started us on a new path to a pulmonologist.

We now have oxygen at our house, and we are ready for those moments when he might need help. The good news is that Graham is not a kid who needs oxygen daily. The better news is that we are now prepared for that emergency situation.

The difficult part is that he needs it at all.

We got oxygen at Graham's school and had the staff there trained on how to use it. We also got suction machines for home and school, in case he vomits. The suction machine is used to clear his mouth of fluid to prevent choking. It works the way a dentist office clears saliva.

Now that he has grown to be a teenager we can no longer turn him to get the vomit out of his mouth. We realized how lucky we have been as we did not have the emergency equipment he might have needed!

As I spoke to the respiratory therapist when she was training us on the oxygen equipment, I asked her about congestive heart failure patients. My mother had a heart attack in January and received oxygen in the hospital, but it did not travel with her. I wondered why and asked what test needed to be given to determine the need for oxygen.

She told me it was an easy test, given at night while she sleeps. Why did her doctor miss this? The staff at the home also missed this? Why was I the one to catch this from out of town? I requested the test from her doctor in April when I visited her. The test showed that she needed oxygen at night. Once again, Graham helped someone through his own experiences. He was proud to know he helped his grandmother.

Mom could clearly not care for herself alone. I did not realize how much she had declined. I had decided to fly to Boston monthly to visit her at the home she had shared with my dad. It was an Alzheimer's facility that we had chosen to support my dad through his illness, and my mom chose to continue to live there in the condo after his death.

There was no medical plan in place to meet my mom's needs, so the staff was not checking in with her regularly to assist with her personal care and attending to her things. Nobody noticed her rapid decline, and it wasn't until I started visiting her monthly that I realized she needed help.

My mother was a hoarder. Not like the TV show...she did not have ten microwaves in unopened boxes. She did, however, have used plastic bags and scraps of paper with scribbled notes on them from the sixties, and she could not throw anything away.

I found expired food, toxic cleansers, and so much garbage it was overwhelming. Clothes, purses, shoes, and jewelry she would never wear again needed to be boxed up and put in storage. Not thrown out or given away. Not until she had passed. She was emotionally attached to her things. I watched her hold a plastic spoon to decide if she needed it or not.

She could not part from it. It was then I knew she was not in control of those thoughts. It felt like that plastic utensil meant more to her than her children.

Fiercely independent, she refused help or involvement from her kids. I respected that until I found her in unsanitary conditions. The meds to keep fluid out of her lungs gave her incontinence problems, and she was soiling herself, covering it up out of shame.

It is challenging to watch your parents age and to see their health decline. It is awful to realize they are not able to care for themselves. I learned that my mother was soiling herself. Daily. She told me she changed her pants daily because urine was running down her leg.

Her Depends could not be properly fitting if urine was running down her legs. It took a few weeks to get her to understand that she needed to find the right fit.

Her answer was to clean her soiled pants. Then she stopped cleaning them and just dried them because she was having so many accidents. She did not know how to ask for help.

She was angry when I tried to help. When I talked to the staff about her daily accidents they were equally upset because they had no idea. They immediately put a plan into place to help her, but my mom declined their attempts to help. Finally the staff came up with a plan to get her soiled clothes from her room when she went to the dining room for meals so that she wouldn't know they were helping her.

I asked them to check to see that she was changing her clothes and not wearing soiled pants anymore. It was horrible. Our roles had reversed. I was parenting my parent.

Around this time I looked under her sink, and it reeked of urine smell. I cleaned it up and realized she could no longer clean. There was no soap in her bathroom, and it was doubtful she was washing her hands. I was leaving for the airport when she asked me a question:

"Do you know what a fungal infection is?"

I put my bag down and went to talk to her.

She showed me her pinky finger that was bright red with infection, the nail was about to fall off. I thought about her urine stained pants, the urine smell under the sink and the lack of soap and realized why she had the infection.

She did not want to go to another doctor. I explained to her that she had to go or she could get very sick with sepsis, if the infection was left untreated.

I went directly to the nurse and alerted her to the infection. I requested that she help explain why my mother had to go to the doctor, and that she made sure she got there. I left with a pit in my stomach. How did she get this bad? How could no one have seen this decline but me? I already had so much on my plate, but there simply was no other answer. I had to help her.

I had an emergency meeting with the home to alert them of her condition. We put a plan into action to care for her and keep her safe and clean without her really knowing much had changed.

To honor her desire to "be in charge," the staff would do what they needed to without her knowledge. Every month I visited, she talked about death. During the first visit she had asked me to rearrange the clothes in her closet and told me which dress she wanted to be buried in.

On the next visit she asked me to read a book about dying and a bible verse about the transition after death. I thanked her and told her I gave the book to a friend whose mom was dying. She told me the bible verse helped her to understand what was happening to her body.

In July 2014, she had heart attack number two and I knew she would not survive it. We drove down to see her in critical care. She laughed, was interacting with her grandchildren and was surrounded by love. She got discharged and died in the ambulance on her way home. You are never prepared for that phone call. All I could do was cry.

She died alone. She never made it home. I cried and cried thinking of this. Later I realized she left on her own terms and she did go home. She was right where she wanted to be, back with my Dad.

Chapter Twenty-six

Beyond the decade
Equipment, testing, and birthdays

What happened a decade later? Here are some of the things we have been working on for the past few years: I had asked a colleague who worked with a person in their twenties what the latest trend was and she told me he worked out with a robotics machine. I did not have high hopes of finding that in Syracuse NY but was pleasantly surprised to find out we did have one.

In 2013 we tried a robotics machine at a rehab place. It was a lot like an Iron Man suit. The machine walked Graham on a treadmill. It was unbelievable to see him move this way. He was amazed at what his body was doing.

We were going twice a week and began to see muscle growth in areas like his wrists and ankles that had never happened before. It was exciting because he is in puberty, and developing muscle growth now is so important for his overall health. It was his "workout."

I got to see a side of him I never knew existed. The competitive side. One day we explained what a personal record was to an athlete. It could be for speed or distance. Suddenly Graham turned to the therapist running the machine and vocalized with a determined look on his face.

"Graham, do you want to go faster"? She asked. He signaled yes with his arm, his head nod and his vocalization.

He demanded it. He broke his own record that day. I got to see him as the determined athlete that he is. How cool.

It was good for him he developed muscles and then insurance denied coverage. So frustrated. Too hard to fight the system to get it changed so we will have to give it up for now. I just can't change it all!

Equipment: Could he use a power chair? We had no idea. There is no power wheelchair training where we live. You can't just put a person in a power chair and expect them to know how to drive it.

It takes skill and that has to be learned. Syracuse is not a big city and we have limited opportunities when it comes to equipment. Everything takes months to order, and there is no one place with lots of chairs to train on to see which one works best.

In 2014 we took him to Pennsylvania to an overnight school to set up power wheelchair training. This school had the facility, staff and equipment available to teach him. He went to the school over February and April breaks and for ESY (Extended School Year) in June of 2014 to do power mobility training.

We had to see if he had the skill or the desire to do this. He got very serious whenever the trip came up. He would get a serious look on his face, and he looked pensive.

He is usually so easy going that it threw me for a loop. I finally realized I needed to talk to him about his feelings. Every day after school Graham and I wheeled under the wisteria vines and read about his day by reading the notes the teachers and therapists wrote in his communication journal. This day was different.

After talking about school for a bit, I told him I wanted to talk about the power wheelchair and what he would be doing over break. I said, "It is hard to learn this skill, and there is no guarantee you will be able to do it."

I needed Graham to hear me say we wanted him to try, just like communicating with a device. It took years to find the right device and years to learn to use it. This was no different. It would take years to learn if he could drive a power chair. It's like an athlete training in their sport.

Most importantly, I needed Graham to know the choice was his. If he could learn to drive it, it was his choice to use a power chair or not. No expectations from us.

When we picked him up after the first break, his therapists said he was driving to learn...not quite learning to drive. He was not focusing on developing skills, more like could he even do it. He was having fun.

His teacher showed us a video of Graham in the power chair. She took him to the gym and told him he could go anywhere he wanted. He drove toward the exit, giggling all the way. We got to see his sense of humor as he began the long road of training.

At the completion of the summer program, the staff was able to tell us with confidence that he had the ability and the desire to use the power chair. However, he would not progress in his skills until he could drive it daily.

Graham is still working on mastering the power chair. He can move forward and stop, but he needs more training before he can move independently. We would have to wait until the following summer at ESY for Graham to be able to drive a power chair daily to see if this is a goal for him in his future.

It's 2015 and after a successful four weeks working at power mobility Graham is doing well enough to start the process to get a chair! Throughout his fifteen years we have constantly tried new things with Graham.

As I think back to all that Graham has been through during his lifetime, it is much more than equipment challenges. Actually it is every test that he has had to endure to this point.

Testing is never easy: It started with blood tests every week. My baby weighed four pounds and I had to get his blood drawn weekly to test the medicine level of the barbiturate that was keeping him from having seizures.

He was so tiny they had trouble finding a vein and I had to help pin him down. He cried throughout and my stomach was in knots. I hated the feeling that I was hurting him.

Then there were eye exams, hearing tests, cat scans, MRI's. Here is a story of one of those tests. So, at age ten, after the Sept 26th seizure scare with Colby, we had scheduled an MRI for Graham. Graham had to be sedated, of course, or he never could have done it. There is something alarming about watching your child be put under with an oxygen mask over his mouth...every time I go through it is the same.

I feel anxious that he will be okay and that he will wake up again, with mixed feelings of concern as you walk out of the room leaving your baby in the hands of strangers. It never gets easier.

This time was hard because the hospital moved his appointment to earlier in the day without telling us. So when I arrived early for his appointment, in their eyes I was late and would have to wait until everyone else was served first. We waited for three hours.

I was unable to give him even a sip of water. I was so emotionally spent by the time he went under that I just sat in the waiting room, hardly moving, texting friends and calling family to pass the time. The MRI took longer than the estimated 45 minutes. I began watching the clock, and my worry was mounting more with each additional five minutes that passed. I called Greg and asked that he come help me get him from recovery; I was physically drained as well.

Dear Graham;

Today you had an MRI to scan your brain. I went in with you and held your hand while the doctor put the mask on your face with the anesthesia. It was scary. They told me it smelled bad, and you didn't like it. I told you not to be scared and to think of the dolphins. Dream of Coral, Kayla, Abacoe and Exhuma.

Coral is Kayla's mom. Kayla has the pink belly. Remember how they jump and play in the water together, and how they touched you with love. Feel that warmth and love, and know we all love you. The doctor has to put a tube down your throat, and I didn't know that. I know you didn't like it when you were intubated as a baby, and I was worried it would be the same thing today.

I promised you I would tell Dr. John and get you to a CST to take the negative energy out of your throat. We need to get rid of any residual drugs used to put you to sleep. Mommy will be doing CranioSacral Therapy as soon as she is able to touch you. I love you so much, and it hurt to watch you be scared.

I didn't want to leave you, but Mommies aren't allowed to stay for the tests. They'll let me see you when you are in recovery. That could take over an hour. Colby and Tysen are here. They are in the waiting room with me and giving me hugs to make me feel better. They love you very much. We all do.

When he had the three day EEG and they put 23 electrodes on his head and wrapped his head with bandages so he looked like a mummy, he took it all in stride. Then at night, he ripped them off. The next day the doctor made the bandages much tighter so he could not escape....not so happy. He is older now and understanding we have to do things we might not like to do, like go to the dentist.

He spooked the dentist one day as he reacted to the gag reflex when they were examining him. The next visit I was told he needed sedated cleaning, and we were discharged. Hmmm. He had made that office uncomfortable. We would find someone else....and we did.

Guess what? He does not need sedated cleaning. He did need someone comfortable with people who have disabilities. We are happy at our new dentist. We shared our story and have helped a lot of local families get dental care for their loved ones.

Some tests work and some do not. We learned a lot about that later as Graham could tell us more about himself. At "Camp" in 2014, he was a rock star, using his device more than ever, advocating for himself, socializing....He got his new hearing aids days before he went to camp.

He had tested differently now that he could confidently communicate and tell us what he heard. His teacher told me he went to "I need" then "sweatshirt," and she realized he was cold. Incredible. Now that he is finally amplified at the right level, he is doing great. No wonder he would flick his hearing aids out of his ears so often. Can you imagine how annoying it would be to be over-amplified?

Just another example of how patient Graham is.

What about birthdays? Many years later, celebrating his birthday would get better. Still hard, but by his 11th birthday I had gone through a lot of transitioning with him. Trying to keep up with his age, I cleaned his room and removed the younger themed items, took a lot of things he does not use away, and rearranged it for an older boy.

His birthday was on a Sunday that year. Tysen was out of town at soccer, Greg and Colby were at a soccer banquet for four hours and then at a game. So it was just the two of us. I invited his grandmother to go to the movies with us. I planned a treat and activity at school for his birthday on the Monday after. Other than that, I had no idea what present to get him or how to make the day special.

The year he turned 13 was going to be the best birthday ever. I planned a party at CHAT Club at Syracuse University. CHAT stood for Communication Hope through Assistive Technology, a program Greg and I founded with Syracuse University's Burton Blatt Institute.

Graham already thought he was pretty cool going up to a college campus. He had met people at BBI that were his friends. It was different because he felt comfortable and happy there. We got into the wheelchair van, and the engine didn't turnover. Oh my god, I thought. It was dead. This could not be happening.

He had to get to SU for this party. Colby was 17 and could drive now, so I asked Colby to take us in his car. He struggled to get the wheelchair in the back, and I held Graham in the front seat, desperate to get there.

"Is this even legal, Mom?"

What was I doing?

"Head back into the driveway," I told Colby. "I am sorry—I never should have done this."

I apologized to Graham and to Colby. Meanwhile, Dad, knowing how important this was to Graham, left work and drove home to jump-start the van and drive us.

We were late, but we made it. His pure joy as his new friends at CHAT sang "Happy Birthday" to him made it all worthwhile. I have truly never seen him happier. He finally had a happy birthday. The pictures say it all.

In 2014, as I wondered how I could ever top last year's birthday, I got an idea. There was a baseball game the night of his 14th birthday. So it was off to the ballpark for us! Graham loves sports. We invited friends, family, and school friends to join us at the game and hit his 14th birthday out of the ballpark!

It was such a great night, and Graham loved seeing his name in lights as the scoreboard wished him a Happy 14th Birthday! That familiar full body smile and squeal of delight showed us that?

At 15, we went back and invited some friends from school. There were fireworks that night. Most people do not get a fireworks show on their birthdays... it was fun!

Chapter Twenty-seven

Beyond court

Graham talks with a computer, and his school "took it down when he didn't answer." A teacher had asked him what he ate for Thanksgiving, which is awful because he does not eat Thanksgiving dinner. He drinks Pediasure and maybe a few bites of pureed food but not turkey or other solid foods.

He could not answer her question because he didn't eat like she did, but she thought it was because he could not use the device. Worse yet, they had taught him that it didn't matter if he did answer or what he said with the device. This jeopardized his desire to use the device.

I thought that Graham would emerge as a communicator when he was 10 years old. Well, when you are wrong, you are wrong. It only took a few weeks into the school year to realize we were in trouble. I realized I had huge problems at school.

I thought it was a personnel or staffing issue at this specific elementary school that proper training would resolve. I naively thought I could effect change at my school or school district. That did not happen. It soon became evident I was in a civil rights battle. This was global perception about disability rights. I could not change a global mindset without help.

This was supposed to be the year Graham emerged as a communicator. My son, Tysen, seeing how upset we were, suggested we go to the movies to get away from the sadness and forget our problems for a while. We went to the movie, "The Help."

I was in tears after viewing the movie, as I realized I was in a civil rights battle for my child to be seen and supported in the way he needed. I realized that I needed to work globally. How in the world was a mom from Manlius (a small town in Central New York) going to do that?

I raised my first two children to walk away from an uncomfortable situation. I could not walk away from this. I taught my boys to find new friends if the ones you were with were not being nice. I could not choose someone new to work with my youngest son.

I was stuck in a negative situation. When I drove up to the parking lot of the school, I would get a pit in my stomach. I would dig deep to find the strength to keep going back. I did not give up. I did not give in. I survived. We both did.

Nothing could change until it went public. I knew then and there that for things to change for my son Graham, I had to tell our stories. It felt just like the movie when the ladies in the south who treated their help the way they did until the stories were told to the public and there was moral outrage.

The first step was to follow school district policy and talk to staff. We talked to everyone we were supposed to and got nowhere. They did not see it our way and we could not change their view. The damage done had regressed my sons' ability to communicate. He shut down.

No one listened to his voice so he stopped trying to communicate. I would have shut down too. There was no other option left but to file a due process law suit against the school district.

Mediation or due process can be a positive experience. Sometimes well- meaning adults do not know the current laws, and it takes this process to bring awareness and change. It took a lawsuit to get Graham the rights the rest of his peers enjoyed daily.

The idea that parents who advocate become targets was true in our situation. After raising the issues and advocating through the process to request changes for our son, the administration took to targeted bullying tactics against our son and our family so far that they tried to send him to a different middle school than the peers he had grown close to in his years at elementary school.

Every 4th grade student goes to the school next door for 5th grade but we got a letter telling us Graham would have to go to another school. What? These kids all knew him. They wanted to send a kid in a wheelchair that talks with an eye gaze computer to a school where he knew no one -why? We felt that they wanted to make us unhappy and punish our child...that's why.

We wasted his whole year with no resolution. The next step was to pull him out of the school that had made him regress with communication and send him to the school in PA, praying he would choose to use his device again to communicate with us after being with kids like him that use devices and seeing that some people actually listen to them!

We pulled Graham out of school in June, and he went to the overnight school for six weeks. We hoped he could overcome this. We cried when he skyped with us, using his device to tell us about "camp " and ask how we were. He did it! Despite all he had been through he did it! He chose communication! We were thrilled.

The law suit was filed in the spring and the case was to be heard over the summer. There were delays out of our control. Time was running out, and our attorneys were forced to take the district to Federal Court so a decision was made before school started in September. It was the best thing that could have ever happened.

We never actually got our official day in court. It was the beginning of telling our story. It hit the papers. I got stopped at Wegman's, at the pharmacy, at the gas station. People who knew me well or barely knew me commented at sporting events or school activities. The community had followed this story, and the feelings were clear.

"We support your effort."

"Keep fighting the fight."

"It shouldn't have to be this hard."

My husband's seventh grade English teacher called, remembering his name and going to the effort to leave us a message of support. We knew then that we had already won.

The judge laughed at the school district's attorney when she tried to argue that they did not want to set a precedent by keeping my son with his peers. "How many kids in wheelchairs that talk with computers are in your district? If an exception isn't the right thing to do here, when is it?" said the judge.

The judge agreed with us and told the school district to make it work. We had won. While there was not an official public ruling in our favor, we were encouraged to work it out through a settlement. We got everything we wanted for Graham and agreed to waive our legal fees and settled the rest of our due process hearing in hopes of Graham settling at one school for the next four years.

We reserved the right to bring back some other concerns at a later date but hoped that a new group of teachers and therapists would mean a new start for all of us. It might not go on the law books to set precedent for others but we got what our son needed which was our goal and that's a win, official or not!

When we were preparing for the case it was challenging to pick what to fight for. There was so much happening that needed to be changed but we had to focus on a few points in order to have a chance of winning. It was so difficult to prioritize and let some things go but we knew our attorney was right to advise us to focus on only a few things at this time.

So, we pushed to have the Speech and Language Pathologist attend monthly team staff meetings. They would not allow her to work directly with Graham but in our settlement she could observe him if invited by the team.

We got two additional meetings focused on Augmentative and Alternative Communication (AAC) needs. This therapist works with so many other local districts and is revered; getting glowing recommendations but our district would not allow her on property without a settlement? Unbelievable!

So I hired Beth to create a daily program for him that summer, to focus on communication and his device for at least one hour a day. She had no time to work with him herself, so she hired people with little to no experience working with devices or special needs persons, proving it can be done.

His summer team was Trish, Jackie, Kelly and Beth. The Summer Olympics occurred that year. It was Graham's own Olympic summer as he worked day in and day out to learn how to use his eye gaze computer voice.

One day while he was working with Kelly and she asked how Graham answers test questions, I realized my son did not know what true or false was. No one had taught him that because no one talked to him like a learner. It was doubtful he had been taught what a test even was. He had never been asked anything but yes and no questions. This hit me like a ton of bricks. I saved my tears for later as the outrage poured through me.

For now I needed a plan to make this fun. I explained that if I said my name is Barb that was a true statement. If I said my hair is purple that was a false statement. Graham giggled. He got it.

The next few weeks we had lots of fun with Trish's kids coming up with silly examples of true/false and teaching Graham how to answer using this method. Then it was on to multiple choice. By the end of the summer he had learned how to answer questions using true/false buttons on his device as well as multiple choice buttons.

In the fall I met with his new school team, presented how he answered questions when tested, and held my breath as I waited to see if they would actually test him. Graham came in to middle school using his computer voice with confidence and never looked back.

He proved to his new team that he was independently using this device to communicate to them, and they got it. He finally had the chance to show what he could do. Could our nightmare really be over? I could not believe it yet. I could not let my guard down. I had been hurt for too long.

A little while later, his first test came home. He was asked three questions, and he answered three questions correctly. I cried. We still had a long way to go, but we were finally on a positive path. I had hope again.

In 2014 his team reported that he scored 100% on a microbiology test. He answered five out of five accurately! Finally, they see what we have known all along!

Seeing him happy and successful made the years of suffering fade away. It took years to distance myself from the pain of being treated unfairly, of my reality that the law could not protect me or my child. Even if NYS ruled in our favor and told our school district to correct the behavior, they could and would break the law again and again.

Beyond civil rights: In September 2011, I faced the same civil rights issues I started with in 2005... but I was a different person. I was no longer alone. Syracuse University started an organization called the Syracuse University Parent Advocacy Center, or SUPAC. Other parents came forward with their struggles.

I had developed boundaries. I had the Individuals with Disabilities Education Act (IDEA) and the Americans with Disabilities Act (ADA) law on my side.

Disability is the last part of segregation this country needs to settle. Simply put, discrimination is a civil rights issue. Again, wow. This is why I had such outrage in Graham's early years. It was moral outrage. He was a person first, and he was not treated that way, just like Black America was not treated that way.

In Brown vs. the Board of Education[1] there is a quote that states, "Next thing you know we'll be allowing handicapped to be integrated."

Are you kidding me?

---

[1] Source: Brown v. Board of Education of Topeka, 347 U.S. 483 (1954).

I had trouble separating my moral outrage and my parental protective nature. It was one and the same to me. I could not change the societal view of my son, but I didn't realize what I was up against either.

Every year we had trouble but I never gave up. Finally the years of stress and pain all came to a screeching halt when information received from New York State was presented publicly: there were sixteen violations of NYS and Federal law in the last four years.

The official acknowledgement that laws were broken and it was not about difficult parents but rather best practices not being followed, made a lot of our pain fade.

There have been many great therapists and teachers who have helped us along the way. There have been situations that were painful but today I focus on helping families work collaboratively to the best of their abilities when things go south.

I began to believe that sharing our stories would help effect change for others.

Chapter Twenty-eight

Beyond CHAT

It was right then that I knew I was meant to tell our stories. To anyone and everyone that would listen. I began telling them, over and over again. It was 12 months later when I was telling my story around a dining room table with a group of women that one of them connected me to a man who could see my vision.

After I shared my story, I was told about Peter Blanck of the Burton Blatt Institute, or BBI, at Syracuse University. They said he was the only other person they had met that spoke with the passion that I did about disability issues. I asked for his email address.

I wrote an email to Peter Blanck. I had never heard of BBI. I was curious. I had been involved at SU in various organizations through the years, but no one had ever referred me to Peter or BBI. Why? I got on the website and figured out why. It was an impressive group working on global and national initiatives and doing amazing work, mostly with adults—and as far as I could tell, much of what they did at that time was out of the Syracuse area, but with projects in New York State and nationally.

I decided to challenge BBI to work in their own backyard. I argued that my son, Graham, and kids like him were their consumers of tomorrow. I had a dream of opening an Augmentative and Alternative Communication or AAC Center here in Central New York. I just wanted a central location that everyone would think of when they heard of a situation with a nonverbal student—a place to start a search for the best individualized communication method.

It took ten years of searching place to place, person to person, tons of travel and devices that did not work to finally find a way for Graham to communicate with his world. Eye gaze technology is what did it for Graham.

There is no one central location to send someone to for the purpose of helping them communicate. There are a lot of agencies or people with pockets of knowledge and equipment. It shouldn't be this difficult. I was determined to make it easier for others. I needed something Peter could not say no to, something do-able.

Graham's Speech and Language Pathologist and I joked that we could host an AAC center in a closet with one light bulb. I seriously asked her, "If I can make this happen, will you run it for me?" She said sure, but I don't think she took me seriously. I told her my idea to pitch BBI on an AAC camp and asked her if she would run it if they said yes. She agreed and wished me luck. Again, I don't think she had much hope.

The connection was immediate, intense, and exciting. The Burton Blatt Institute was doing cutting edge projects nationally and globally, and yet in their own backyard I had been struggling for 12 years. I presented an idea for a one week summer camp for nonverbal children using devices to communicate. Peter agreed. He heard my words: "There is nothing out there for this age group or this community of nonverbal persons of this magnitude.

"THEY SAID YES!!!!

Communication Hope through Assistive Technology, or CHAT Camp, was pitched to Peter at a lunch meeting on November 27, 2012. It was my birthday. For months I had seen 11:27 on clocks, phones, computers....it was odd, but it kept happening. I knew it was a sign. I know today it was a significant moment for me. It was the beginning of something bigger. I still see 11:27 on clocks and it's been three years now, reminding me that this movement was meant to be!

I pitched the camp to Peter and told him I would find the campers and that I had a director to run it. He asked me to consider financially contributing to BBI to fund the camp. Done. We set up a meeting with the director and others to fine tune a plan. It was a conscious choice to host a pilot. We chose to avoid research and all the hoops to jump through that came with it.

We recruited five campers. Five kids of all ages, abilities and devices. They used five different ways to communicate. We opened people's eyes and minds. We showed the world how these kids communicate. We touched lives. We started a movement!

Our youngest camper was a little boy who used an iPad to talk. The next camper was medically fragile and came with a nurse and oxygen. Her smile with the football players made everyone melt. She used a switch to activate her voice. The third camper used a dynovox, another AAC device. Graham was the only middle school student using eye gaze technology to talk.

Our oldest camper was in high school and could use his voice in a limited way. He learned to use an iPad that week. BBI is set up as a national and internationally-connected not for profit and is positioned to take an initiative global.

The timing of my connection to BBI was uncanny. Peter was writing a book about "eQuality" and assistive technology, and there were several projects including research that a BBI project like CHAT immediately tied into. Very quickly I found myself with an SU email account, an office at BBI, and in multiple meetings planning and brainstorming about how CHAT impacted their current work. Pinch me.

I was interviewed by the Daily Orange, the student-run newspaper at Syracuse University. Pinch me again. I explained to the young reporter that would be covering this story, she would be helping us to spread awareness that everyone communicates differently. It had an impact on her. She was proud to help effect change in her own small way.

On the final day of CHAT Camp, we held a CHAT Celebration. Here are a few of the words from my presentation:

"Many families in our world have non-verbal family members. Learning to listen to how each of them communicates differently can be challenging. Allowing technology to assist them to open their voices to the world is also challenging.

Communication Hope through Assistive Technology, or CHAT, has brought awareness to our community. Our very own CHAT pack, the fantastic five pilot campers you meet today, have truly redefined the word 'communication.' You lead by example! Thank you!"

I am now able to tell my stories to the world. Through the Burton Blatt Institute at Syracuse University I have been working on global change in disability awareness with regard to communication. My stories are helping people all over the world understand that we all communicate differently. I hope it will never take another family more than a decade to reach and communicate with their child.

CHAT Camp was a huge success. As we regrouped to determine the feasibility of continuing, Beth Tollar, the camp director, and I agreed that this experience was too overwhelming for us personally. The reality was that BBI needed to create a budget line for it to be sustainable, and without additional sponsors and funding it could not continue the project. We approached several national funders, but no takers.

We then reasoned that a CHAT Club would be easier to replicate and came up with a plan to host one in a community agency for a few months to see if it was replicable.

Our way to introduce our campers to the SU campus was to create a fun social group at BBI, and we called it CHAT Club. The goal was to have each of the campers go and meet at least one or two of the campers so it would not be scary on the first day of camp, and we tried the same thing in the community

During the CHAT Celebration, AccessCNY (known as Enable/TLS at that time) approached me and offered to support CHAT in any way they could, and so we met to discuss a pilot hosted at their agency. We submitted a grant request to a local foundation. BBI wrote a letter of support for Enable/TLS to get this grant to see if we could run a self - sustaining club.

The spring of 2014 was chosen, and CHAT Club pilot again was a great success. Through outreach on CHAT Central (the first-ever accessible website for non-verbal kids like Graham to interact with each other), and real life connections (AAC camp piloted in August 2013, CHAT Club pilot at Enable/TLS spring of 2014), CHAT had already changed lives. I achieved every goal I set for CHAT Camp and CHAT Club. It was time for some new goals and a new direction.

The next part of our journey, Graham's and mine, is to share our story with the world. Peter and the CHAT committee all told me that when I spoke at the CHAT Celebration it was like hearing an evangelist...you could feel the excitement in the room. People believed in the passion of my stories and the conviction I have to tell the world.

I had to determine what it was about me and my story that was different. I realized that my passion and experience are what drives this vision.

I know now that the next step in my journey is the development of a new company: CHAT Collective. So, I created a company that would shift the dynamic of how the world communicates with each other because I believe that everyone can communicate! I am passionately working to change the mindset of the verbal community. My hope is that telling our stories will do just that.

Chapter Twenty-nine

Beyond the fear of his death

There are so many times that I faced Graham's death. The thought or reality that my child might die right then and there is something most people cannot fathom. There is no way you could understand the fear, the adrenaline rush, the emotional hell this brings until you have felt it yourself. I hope you never experience that.

For those of you who have been there, I get it. A life threatening episode of a seizure, choking on vomit, gasping for air needing oxygen. Whatever the situation, it takes a physical and emotional toll. Just as I was finishing this book, it happened again only this time I was all alone. Greg was with Tysen in Virginia at the UVA orientation so there was no one in the house to help me with Graham.

I heard the sound while I was watching TV. It's a muffled choking sound that sent chills through my spine because I knew what it meant. He was vomiting, he could not clear his airway and I had minutes to get to him. I ran up the stairs, grabbed the suction machine and used all my strength to lift his back and head up so he would not choke. I had to get the vomit out of his mouth as fast as I could...but something was wrong. It wasn't working. The machine was not working.

My mind raced with options...do I call 911? There isn't time... he might die before they got here. Then I remembered there was a machine that went to and from school downstairs. I flew down those stairs, grabbed the machine yelling to Graham that it would be okay I was almost there. Over and over I kept thinking don't die, not now, not while I am alone with you, please....

It worked and I began to clear his airway, his mouth. When I was able to focus on the scene he was covered in vomit. It was all over his pajamas, his bedding...he was a mess. It was not stopping. It had been a good ten minutes and I was starting to panic.

Now I was yelling to Graham that he had to hang on, make it through this, that we could do it together. I wasn't ready for him to die (who would ever be ready for that?) and the fighter in me kicked into gear... not now I thought.

I knew I could not keep this up for much longer. The hard cold reality that I could not help him much longer set in. I hated that I could not do this myself. I was terrified that my ego would get in the way of saving him and I realized that I needed help. I dropped the suction, ran for the phone and called 911.

They could hear him choking/coughing as I tried to make sense through my tears. When they asked for my address I gave them one I lived at 20 years ago... stress does funny things. The operator calmly said it did not match the phone number and could I give that address again...what in the world?

I quickly told him our address then hung up and called my in-laws to come over (they lived ten minutes away) and then called Greg in Virginia. I did not call him first because they were here and could be driving to me while I talked to him. I also weirdly felt like I failed Graham because I had to call for help. If Greg was here I would not have called. If Greg were here alone, he would not have had to call. I had to face that I needed help.

I ran downstairs to open the door and ran back upstairs to continue suction. Then surprisingly he stopped. The ambulance had not arrived yet and there was a moment of quiet. It was either the calm before the storm or we had weathered the worst part of the storm. Very soon six rescue workers entered the bedroom ready to help, but seeing that things were quiet, asked what was happening and what I wanted them to do.

I explained what had taken place and asked them to stay. Graham had a vacant look on his face and we wondered if he had a seizure but there was no way to know if that happened while he was alone because he could not tell us.

I thought back to earlier when he got home from summer camp earlier that day. He was tired and I put him in bed to relax but he crashed and slept for five hours, which is very unusual behavior for him. I wondered again if he was fighting a stomach bug or if he had a seizure. Back to the moment at hand.

I had to change him and clean the bedding but I knew when I moved him he might start vomiting again...and he did. They let me suction him, listened to his lungs to make sure there was no fluid in them, reassuring me that it was okay.

We did not need to go to the hospital that night because Graham rallied, but I could not have known that was how it would play out. I started to cry tears of relief and they asked if I was okay. I thanked them for being there for us and let them know they could go, we would be okay.

At 1:30am I posted on Facebook. Unable to sleep and scared by my experience I reached out for comfort and am so grateful to the many wonderful friends and family members that connected with me, sending love, healing and prayers our way. I no longer felt alone.

The next day when I was talking to a friend who has faced life threatening episodes with her child as well, we wistfully wished we didn't have to think of their deaths, that it would be so nice to have that life that other families have filled with vacations to the beach and fun memories. Instead we had memoires of poop, vomit and fear.

There are wonderful memories too. It's not all bad, it's just really hard to focus on the good times because the bad ones happen every year and sometimes more than once a year and are so very frightening it is hard to recover. You pick up the pieces, put a smile on your face and go on. You just go on.

I remember one night as we were in the process of helping Colby with college applications I was clearing the dinner table, joking with Graham about it. "What a surprise; everyone left the dishes for mom," I said. He giggled. Then, the unexpected happened.

Using an eye gaze computer to talk, on March 8, 2013, my son said, "I love you." A synthetic computer voice, out of nowhere, said the words I never thought I would hear from Graham. Tears streamed down my face. I was so proud of him, so full of love, yet so confused. I didn't even know he had the words programmed on his device. It was a pivotal moment. I knew it and Graham knew it.

He found a way to give me that gift, and he was so proud of himself! He was wearing a t-shirt that said "Too much awesome," and he had a great big smile on his face. Awesome is right!

The fall of 2014 would prove to be incredible as Graham showed his communication skills, teaching others that he could communicate by cheering at a soccer game. At one of the first games of the season he went to his colors page and said, "Green, green, green."

Our school colors are green and white. Fans often cheer, "Go green." I realized Graham wanted to cheer, and we had to program a cheer page for him. Graham's big brother, Tysen, was the captain of the team, and he was very proud of him.

The next game he cheered for two hours straight. I was blown away. He said everything there, over and over again. The people at the game were amazed to hear his voice. They learned that he could independently communicate.

One game he was cheering for Tysen when he was not on the field. Tysen had already scored five goals and was not going to be playing anymore, but I realized Graham could not see that he was not playing. So I told him not to cheer for his brother but explained what his other options were.

He immediately used the other cheers and once again, people in the crowd were amazed to hear him choose the other options and continue to cheer and support the team.

Another game we were down 1-0, and no one was cheering for our team. Suddenly his synthetic computer voice yelled, "I want to win" and the fans started cheering with him: "I want to win too, Graham!" Within minutes his brother scored a goal to tie the game. The goal was exciting, but hearing Graham lead the fans cheering was more exciting. I still get the chills as I tell that story. He is a confident communicator today.

Chapter Thirty

Beyond transitions

No one prepares you for how difficult it is when your children grow up and graduate from high school. It started for me during the Junior year with my oldest son Colby. I just got sad.

I would spontaneously cry about random things... seeing a mother and a baby and realizing I would never be that young mother again, that those days of babies are over.

We sat on the monorail at Disney and I cried thinking of all the past trips we had with memories of my little boys flashing before me. I wanted it to stop. The boys were embarrassed that I would burst into tears in public and so was I. Worse, I was in emotional pain and it was out of control.

When Colby went off to college he stopped talking to me. That is how it felt to me at least. I did not realize how much we spoke until it ended. If I texted or called I got a brief answer and then silence.

It was so hard to just stop communicating with him every day and yet I realized that I would not have wanted a friend or a boyfriend who talked to his mother all the time. It just hurt to be the one that was cast away.

What made things worse is that Colby called and texted Greg more than he did his whole life. His dad is an engineer and could answer questions or talk about his new classes and I didn't understand that world. It felt to me like they talked every day sometimes more than once. The calls were brief but it didn't matter to me. It was so painful.

I actually asked Greg to stop telling me that he called. It hurt less if I did not know they spoke. Colby called me to discuss what he called the more important things. I am sure he had no idea that the calls to his dad outnumbered the calls to mom or that might be hard for me.

I remember one night at dinner Tysen told us to stop all the attention on him. "I know you miss Colby but this is too much for me" he said. We laughed, but he was right. We focused on Tysen more than we should have. We tried to back off.

Soon it was Tysen's senior year and soccer began... then we would be faced with all the "lasts" of high school for Tysen. Here come the tears again. I am not ready for him to leave this house too. It would just be Greg, Graham and I this fall and I was dreading it.

I was busy starting a new company, but the sadness was always there. So what is next for me? Golf! Golf was a big part of my life before I had kids. I resented golf when I was growing up because my parents spent more time on the golf course than they did with me.

My husband Greg and I started to learn the sport together after we were married. Ironically we then spent more time with my parents as we could golf together in a foursome. Through the years we played in many golf tournaments with my parents in Boston, Syracuse and Arizona.

When my first child was born my mother in law sat for him once a week so I could golf. I met my pediatrician on the golf course when I was pregnant! I dropped 10 strokes off my game during pregnancy as nature adjusted my stance. Greg and I did a lot of social events at our golf club and had many friends there.

After Graham was born we were in crisis mode and golf disappeared from our lives. We tried to get out there occasionally but our time was limited and we were overwhelmed with three kids and all the therapy that came with Graham. I was golfing with a friend who was just learning to play one day when I felt my back twinge after I drove my ball off the first tee.

It hurt like a sharp pain and I felt fear of really hurting myself. I had to be physically fit to care for Graham. I picked my ball up and never swung again. There was no choice. I gave up golf for Graham.

In 2015 my son Tysen asked me why I gave golf up. He pointed out that I do not have to lift Graham anymore because I use a lift and asked if I thought I would start playing again. It hadn't occurred to me. It had been over a decade since I competitively played. Could I still do it? Did I want to golf again?

I mulled it over for several weeks. My life was changing. My boys are all older and hardly spend time with me anymore. I used to be the center of their worlds (they would never agree with that statement). I was out of a job and I didn't like it at all. Golf would be something we could do together. That was compelling enough to get me to the range to try it.

If I could do it, this would provide an opportunity for a new relationship with Colby and Tysen. So Greg got my clubs out of our storage area and it had holes in the bag with mice droppings falling out... yuck. The clubs were old and chipped but they would work.

I did not have a putter, shoes or a glove but I did have a positive attitude. I borrowed a putter from the pro shop and beat Tysen in a putting match for fun. We went to the range and I was hitting okay. My clubs were old and outdated but I could play so I signed up for a few lessons and started the road back.

I did not realize how much golf played a part in my relationship with Greg. There really was no time to do anything together outside of caring for Graham, Colby and Tysen. Our relationship revolved around our children, which was not ideal.

I joined the league to give myself time. It sounds strange but it was really hard to gift myself this time. I chose to start golfing again to connect with my children. Gratefully the skills came back decently and while my scores are high there are some great shots that keep me hopeful. I have the potential to play better if I stick with it.

This fall Tysen started college and Greg and I are home with Graham. Life forces transitions and this is one of them. While Graham is at school, maybe I can golf. Empty nesting is what people call this. It's a time of grieving. Even though Graham is with us it is different. He is different.

When the other boys were here we focused on all of their activities and Graham was a part of it all. Without the boys home, our attention is on Graham and all that is different for him and that hit us hard.

That part of my life is over. I will not have little children in my house until the day my boys marry and have kids of their own (so not ready to be a grandmother yet!) It makes me sad when I look back at pictures of our family life and all we did when our kids were growing up. I have started to take them down and pack away the memories. It is too painful to look at the past.

Chapter Thirty-one

Beyond expectations

I was not going to be a parent that got stuck in the anger, pain, or suffering. I had no idea how many times my family would be thrown into life threatening, stressful situations full of pain and hurt. I held true to my conviction to move through it and always found a way. I made a conscious decision early in life to not get stuck in the negative stuff.

I heard a parent of a 25 year old speak about their experience in the Neo-Natal Intensive Care Unit (NICU), and she was as angry as if it had just happened to her. I had helped start a support group but realized that night that I did not fit in.

In life, we make ourselves sad when our expectations are not met. It is difficult to remember Deepak Chopra's advice to live in the moment or to understand the power of right now. We set ourselves up by hoping things will turn out a certain way. Sometimes we are happy, our expectations are met and life goes on. Other times, it doesn't go that well.

So how do we adjust? How do you accept disappointment? Things do not always go the way you hope they would. Realistically, we know it cannot always go the way we want it to go. Yet, try to explain to a child of thirteen that he needs to "roll with it." Does he? Does he need to roll with it?

When do we learn the lesson of life that part of life is disappointment? Who teaches us that when things don't go your way, you can't just have a temper tantrum? Is it the job of the adult in your life? There are tons of adults who still need that lesson...they are still throwing temper tantrums.

Maybe life itself teaches us and reteaches us this lesson in varied ways every year of living. Are you open to hear this lesson?

When do you learn to differentiate between acceptance and being stuck? Who helps you piece together the things that you can move through? For me, this knowledge came in many ways.

CranioSacral Therapy (CST) helped me on a journey of personal development. I was empowered first to see and accept patterns in my life that were undesirable or unhealthy, then to make a shift to change the pattern.

I put myself through school in my forties to start on a new path, one that I have foreseen since I was a child. When asked what I wanted to be when I grew up I always answered, "I want to help people."

The all-knowing adults in my life told me I needed to pick a real job. Where was the support? Who was listening to what I wanted? Why didn't anyone help me figure out how to help people? Instead my voice was silenced. My dreams buried.

Years later, I found my way back to that dream. I would find my way through the Upledger Institute learning CranioSacral Therapy. I put myself through school to get a license as a massage therapist in New York State. I held onto my dream to do the work that had helped Graham.

I founded my own business, Ultimate Yu, and gave back this gift that had been given to me. It doesn't get any more real than this. My company's name, Ultimate Yu, is the name created by a friend that received work and understood that the experience is different for each person. No session has ever been the same for me. Each session is unique and it truly is all about you. Ultimate Yu. Be Better.

At the opening celebration for my first business in 2010, my friend in real estate said to me "this is exactly what you described to me the first day we met." If you have ever read the book "The Secret," I put it out there and it happened.

To me, becoming a CranioSacral Therapist meant adopting the beliefs that I learned from my journey with multiple therapists and CST: we believe people are self - healing. We provide a healing space for you to discover the process with an intention to honor the human body, to love and respect yourself and each other and to live in the moment, appreciating all that life has to offer.

My clients have given me everything I dreamed of, and as I look back at my goals from the first day of massage school, I have achieved them all. I was able to help hundreds of people and return the gift of healing that I had received.

If you are one of the many clients I have interacted with through the years I am honored to have connected with you. To be present when you faced your fears or the challenges life delivered including disappointment, abandonment, grief, death, disease, dysfunction, concussions, car accidents, stroke, cancer, murder, rape, disability, cults, so many varied situations that landed on my doorstep through my clients. I am grateful to have been one small step in your path to healing. And I honor everyone who has helped me as well.

Epilogue:

Beyond hope: a journey

We are on display everywhere we go, teaching the world that there are different ways to communicate. Most people were unable to envision this happening. It was too much. How can a child communicate without words?

It's part of why I am telling the story. It's been a lifetime of experience, heartache, heartbreak, celebrations and happy moments all mixed together so that life became a moment-to-moment thing.

Graham found his voice to speak to the world. Silently communicating, teaching without words, it is now time to emerge. I never gave up on reaching him. Graham continues to amaze people as he communicates with an eye gaze computer.

I have always known Graham is cognitively able. When we found CranioSacral Therapy (CST) I began to see that those therapists could see it too. It then became very confusing, as in one world (CST) he was revered as an old soul, a teacher.

He connected with John Upledger himself, who told me he came to this world to me in this form for a reason. That he was here to teach us all the lessons we needed to learn. I heard the words but wondered how that could be when the teachers and therapists at Graham's school did not see that at all.

Worse yet, they were saying things like "He can't hear you—I don't know why you bother talking to him" or "He doesn't want to walk—you might as well take this walker back home."

They would ask him a question he just answered correctly five times in a row. He stopped answering, of course. (Wouldn't you?) When I asked why the teacher asked him the same question five times, her answer was "to be sure." This form of torture continued for Graham. His answers were never heard.

Another therapist graded him as mastering a skill one quarter and then the next quarter she marked him as slowly progressing in that same skill. When I asked why she was still working on a skill he had mastered, she answered, "Kids like Graham can pass one minute and fail the next."

I felt like I was in a bad movie, but it was really happening to him. So in her eyes, he would never pass anything. He was judged incapable of any progress.

Yet in his other world (CST), people around the world were so touched by him that they had his picture on their office walls, and they lectured about him in pediatrics classes taught internationally.

He was featured in the Upledger Institute newsletter, *Massage and Body Work Magazine,* a national publication. None of this made sense. It was like two polar worlds, and we existed in both. One hell—and he suffered daily in it, and we were unable to help him.

In the other world, he was a celebrity. A healer in his own right. I watched as he taught therapists how to work with him. I often heard, "Oh you want me to work there?" or "Thanks for showing me that" or "Graham is a great teacher" or "Graham is amazing" or "Graham got it about 15 seconds before every therapist in this room, he is way ahead of all of us."

When I look back and wonder how I got through it, I guess I just opened myself to experience everything. I survived it, and so did Graham. But why?

To share it with the world and offer hope to those children and families out there who suffer daily like we did.

Dr. John became like a father to me. He allowed me to take his courses without a license to touch as long as I signed a waiver not to use CST on anyone for a fee. I could use it with family and friends, and Graham.

One trip I asked him how you learn to work with the dolphins. He winked at me and told me he knew someone who might be able to arrange that.

He encouraged me to apply to take the highest level of classes, the Advanced CST course. You could only continue if you had his permission. He read the application letters himself, and I was approved. After Advanced I continued on with Bio Aquatics so I could work with the dolphins.

I experienced the joy of seeing other parents see their child empowered in their own healing process, or do something new for the first time ever, or hope in their eyes where there was none before. I have deep gratitude and love for John Upledger (Papa John) for loving us, teaching us and giving a gift to this world that makes it "one touch better" (something he said often).

I knew the last time I saw my dad, and I knew the last time I saw Dr. John. They died the same year within a few months of each other. I grieved them both when they were alive losing each to Alzheimer's or dementia. The physical body was still around, but the connection to the man I knew was lost. Then, when the physical body passed, I grieved them both again.

I wrote a letter to Dr. John: "There were no words to describe how I felt after our sessions. 'Thank you' was all that came out, but it wasn't enough. It was the feeling in the room. Indescribable."

Today if I could, I would say to Dr. John: "You taught me how to love myself and to feel and know when I connect with someone. To let it happen, and to enjoy it. It was like an awakening. To life, to love, in ways I hadn't known before. 'Follow your heart. Let your heart be happy,' you told me. It truly is. Thank you, Papa John!"

Most of us never know the love that Graham does. Don't feel sorry for Graham, feel the Graham connection.

Sure, he has challenges in every part of his life; but he can connect with people on a level so deep that most of us will never feel. I have seen him change a person's mood and affect people with love and joy. It is a gift to witness. It is a bigger gift to be on the receiving end of his gift to our world.

Many have described him as an old soul, wise beyond his years, an indigo child, a teacher...wondering how many past lives he has had and why he came to this world in this form. His radiant smile gets a smile in return from even the grouchiest of souls.

His giggle or belly laugh leave lasting impressions, and even in the story about what happened to him you can see and feel the joy that he imparted to those present. Graham's giggle was included in a meditation CD released in 2005 because one of the therapists was so moved by his laughter.

As Graham has grown, so has my own reflection and awareness. Now I live in the moment and appreciate things I never did before. I found a connection with others that strive for inner peace and balance, and it's now hard to exist in both worlds.

I could never have known back in 2005 what this journey would be like. I would go through an emotional roller coaster of pain for over a decade and somehow find the strength to face it all and survive. Challenges would come from every aspect of my life and Graham's: health, family, school, communication, illness, death...

To quote Ilchi Lee, author of The Call of Sedona: Journey of the Heart: "Even when it encounters an obstacle, flowing water always goes on its intended way. If it meets a rock, even if it parts, it goes around and around again and keeps flowing. If there is no path, it makes one."

I was put on this path by the dolphins, John Upledger, and CranioSacral Therapy. I have accepted my sense of knowing as coming from the universe. I believe we are all connected, and if you open up your heart to whatever might appear, you will be guided by that connection.

I am grateful to the universe for giving me the tools to be like flowing water and find my way, or make a new path. At this moment, right now, all is well in my world.

When I started to write this book in 2010 it was daunting. I relived the emotions and it was going to take too long to finish it so I got the idea to create a video to share our stories while I was writing. Here are some excerpts from the video I produced in 2011. To see the video go to my website: ***www.chatcollective.com***

Colby: "Graham taught me to accept people at face value, not judging or coming into a conversation with prejudices or stereotypes."

Tysen: "My little brother faces many challenges because he has cerebral palsy."

Colby: "I've seen people stare at him for as long as ten seconds. It breaks my heart."

Tysen: "He can light up the room with his amazing smile and intelligence."

Colby: "He has taught me that even a child that struggles to make noise can have a brilliant smile and light up a room."

Mom and Dad: "Life is about our connection with others; connection with family...connection with his brothers."

Tysen: "My brother has helped me get through so many hard times. Despite all the negative odds, he still has a positive attitude."

Tysen: "My brother Graham is getting better at walking, talking, and everything that is hard for him. That is why I am lucky."

Mom and Dad: "Connection with his school, connection with his community..."

Colby: "When my brother was born, I realized that everyone was different--but that everyone was the same inside."

Colby: "He himself defies the stereotypes. He is the single best thing to have happened in my life. He cannot walk and he cannot talk--yet we in my family understand him just the same."

Tysen: "I rise above it all, defeating the challenges I face, persevering over it all. I am able."

Colby: "Are people like Graham really that different than you and I? A disability is a mask for some people. They judge the mask and not the person."

Mom and Dad: "Because of Graham we try harder, we give further and we forgive sooner. We live simpler, thank easier, hope longer. We love deeper, and we laugh louder."

Tysen: "Always be strong, and don't let anyone bring you down. Be the best that you can be."

Colby: "The conclusion that I have come to is that people are afraid of what they don't know."

About the Author

Barbara Huntress Tresness is an author, disability advocate and founder of CHAT Collective and Ultimate Yu. Her son Graham serves as the inspiration for all of her writing. As a result of a life changing occurrence at the Upledger Institute where she and Graham were part of the dolphin assisted therapy program, Barb began a healing journey and became a certified craniosacral therapist with the Upledger Institute. She started Ultimate Yu with the desire to give back the gift of CST that her family benefited from, and has helped hundreds of clients on their healing journey with craniosacral therapy.

Barb's journey to becoming a leading advocate for Nonverbal and Limited Communicators began when her son, Graham, was born with Cerebral Palsy. She witnessed firsthand the challenges of a community poorly equipped to meet the needs of a nonverbal child. Therefore, she embarked upon a worldwide search for techniques, technologies and treatments to help Graham and others with limited communication skills.

Graham has touched many lives and telling his story has become her life work. As an advocate, expert, and national speaker, Barb is on a mission to give the gift of communication and hope to the world.

Barb is passionate about revolutionizing the way the verbal community socializes and communicates with people that have communication challenges. She founded CHAT Collective and has developed communication tools, techniques and also written *Everyone Communicates: Learn How to Talk to Me! - The guidebook to communicating and socializing with Non Verbal Communicators (NVC's) and Limited Communicators (LC's).*

She received a Bachelor of Arts from the University of Vermont, and currently lives with her husband and three sons in Manlius, New York. You can connect with Barb at *www.barbarahuntresstresness.com,* on Facebook and at *www.chatcollective.com.*

Acknowledgements

I would like to thank all of you who contributed to this book through our connections and experiences on this crazy roller coaster ride we call life. Whenever or however we met, you touched our lives and we are grateful.

To Colby, Tysen and Graham I could not have imagined the love you brought to my life.

To Beth Tollar: Thank you for opening your heart to our family and sharing your family with us. Your ability to work with people with communication challenges changed our lives.

To Kate Battoe: I treasure our friendship and feel a special connection to you that leaves me smiling and happy every time we are together. Thank you for your first round of edits of this manuscript and for many moments of fun!

To Lydia Johnson Grandy: Thank you for years of creativity and fun developing so many wonderful projects together. You are a gift to many who know you!

To my brother Bill Huntress: Thanks for being you! You are such a big part of Graham's enjoyment in the fantasy football league... you have a special relationship that is so wonderful to see. I wish you much happiness.

To Laura Ponticello: For your divine guidance and support. I am grateful that we connected and deeply appreciate your talents and gifts to our world.

To Peter Blanck Chairman of the Burton Blatt Institute at Syracuse University: Thank you for believing! From the first time we met you believed in me, and encouraged me to share my stories with the world. CHAT in all its forms, has been a gift we have shared together.

To Dr. John Upledger: Thank you for loving Graham, loving me, and for developing craniosacral therapy which has impacted hundreds of thousands of lives, making them one touch better. CST changed our lives and so did you! You told me I would help a lot of people like Graham one day, and I hope this book does just that.

To the many clients who shared their inner journeys and had the courage to face adversity head on and allow me to be a silent witness to that, I honor you.

To the many therapists who gifted me their time and love as I took my own journey of healing, I am grateful.

To the dolphins: Your mystical wisdom and love both healed and guided us to be who we are today.

To Mary and Andy Tresness: For all the love and support you have showed me through the years.

To my husband Greg: For a wonderful life together. For being my partner on this wild roller-coaster life filled with ups and downs. When we met at college when we were 18 years old, I could never have imagined the years of happiness we would have together raising a family and seeing our boys grow to be successful young men.

With gratitude and love,
Barb

order at www.divinephoenixbooks.com

www.pegasusbooks.net

and the author's website:
www.chatcollective.com
www.barbarahuntresstreness.com

CPSIA information can be obtained at www.ICGtesting.com
Printed in the USA
BVOW11s0050200116

433544BV00003B/4/P